Vegetarian

Vegetarian

Sue Ashworth

Carole Handslip

Kathryn Hawkins

Cara Hobday

Jenny Stacey

Rosemary Wadey

Pamela Westland

p

This is a Parragon book
This edition published in 2001

Parragon
Queen Street House
4 Queen Street
Bath, BA1 1HE UK

Copyright © Parragon 1998

ISBN: 0-75256-669-5 (Hardback)
ISBN: 0-75256-665-2 (Paperback)

Printed in China

Edited, designed and produced by Haldane Mason, London

Update and cover design by The Bridgewater Book Company

Acknowledgements
Editor: Jo-Ann Cox
Editorial Assistant: Elizabeth Towers
Design: dap ltd
Photographers: Karl Adamson, Sue Atkinson, Iain Bagwell, Amanda Heywood,
Joff Lee, Patrick McLeavey, Clive Streeter, Andrew Sydenham
Home Economists: Sue Ashworth, Sue Atkinson, Carole Handslip, Kathryn Hawkins,
Cara Hobday, Louise Pickford, Rosemary Wadey

Note
Tablespoons are assumed to be 15 ml. Unless otherwise stated, milk is assumed to be
full-fat, eggs are medium and pepper is freshly ground black pepper.

Contents

Bakes & Roasts 144

Side Dishes & Salads 168

Desserts 198

Introduction

People choose to eat vegetarian food for all sorts of different reasons, whether on moral grounds, for health reasons, for economy or simply because they prefer the flavour. Whatever the motive, one thing is certain – everyone enjoys good food, and vegetarian food can be as good as, and indeed often better than, traditional meat and fish dishes. Vegetarian meals are perfect for entertaining or just for the family to enjoy, and can be easily adapted to suit all tastes.

This inspirational cookbook is designed to appeal to vegetarians and vegans alike as it contains a wide range of recipes which will appeal to all. Another aim is to dispel the myth that vegetarian food is brown, stodgy and bland. When browsing through the recipes you will discover just how versatile, colourful and flavourful a vegetarian diet can be. It makes perfect sense when you consider the natural foods used and the wide range of produce available all year round, all of which are suitable for the vegetarian diet.

With the advent of refrigerated transport, fresh produce is now shipped from all over the world to give us a whole array of fresh fruit and vegetables with which to create delicious recipes. The use of exotic spices, fresh herbs and garlic, sauces and relishes makes for an exciting and healthy diet.

Eating a balanced, healthy diet is very important. This can be easily achieved by combining the different recipes in this book when planning your meal, to include protein, carbohydrate, vitamins, minerals and some fats. It is very important in any diet, but especially a vegetarian diet, that a good balance is achieved and that sufficient protein is eaten, and you should bear this in mind when deciding which of the wonderful recipes to try in the chapters that follow.

When it comes to recipes, there are dishes from far and wide, including the Orient, Middle East and the Mediterranean. The diets in these regions are healthy and the native ingredients and flavourings are exciting and delicious. The book also contains more familiar recipes and variations on themes, such as Vegetable Toad-in-the-Hole, a quick, tasty family meal in which I guarantee that the meat won't be missed. Indeed, this can be said for all of the recipes in this book. Many could be served to meat-eating guests without them missing the 'meat factor' in any way. It is the perfect way to introduce your friends to this healthy and delicious diet.

When cooking the following recipes, feel free to substitute some of the ingredients to suit specific diets, using soya milk, for example, instead of cow's milk, cream substitute instead of the dairy cream and vegetarian margarine instead of butter. In this way you will enjoy a whole range of super starters, tasty light meals and snacks, wonderful main meals and accompaniments, and delicious desserts. This cookbook will allow you to discover or reaffirm that the vegetarian diet has progressed greatly from the nut cutlet to a colourful and imaginative way of eating. Enjoy!

VEGETARIAN NUTRITION

Vegetarian food is extremely healthy, and can provide all the important vitamins, minerals, proteins, carbohydrates and fats that make up a nutritious, well-balanced diet. And because more fruit, vegetables, grains and pulses tend to be eaten, the diet is rich in complex carbohydrates, the primary source of energy and fibre, which helps to keep the body vibrant and healthy.

Protein

Obtaining sufficient protein is not a problem in a vegetarian diet as there are plenty of foods from which to choose. Eggs, cheese, milk, nuts, beans and soya products, such as TVP (texturized vegetable protein), soya milk, tofu or Quorn, are all excellent sources. Make sure that you eat a wide variety of these foods to get the full range of protein that your body needs.

Fat

Another additional benefit of following a vegetarian diet is that it can be quite low in fat. The main sources of fat in your diet will be from vegetable, nut and olive oils, dairy foods, nuts and any products containing these ingredients. So slimmers can succeed in losing weight following a vegetarian diet, provided they keep an eye on their overall fat intake.

Carbohydrates

A vegetarian diet is rich in complex carbohydrates, found in starchy foods, such as brown rice, oats, and wholewheat pasta and bread. These are particularly useful to dieters, as they ensure a steady release of energy and a stable blood sugar level.

Vitamins

Fruit and vegetables are packed with important vitamins, essential for our general well-being and the healthy functioning of our bodies. If you follow a vegetarian diet, you can't go far wrong.

The best sources of vitamin A are yellow fruits and vegetables and some green vegetables – apricots, peaches, spinach and carrots, for example. It is also present in butter and added to margarines. Vitamin A helps us to resist infections and keeps the skin, hair, eyes and body tissues in healthy condition.

The B group vitamins act as a catalyst in the releasing of energy from food. They are also vital for the maintenance of a healthy nervous system and red blood cells. Apart from vitamin B12, all the B vitamins can be found in yeast and wholegrain cereals, especially wheat flour and wheatgerm. Vegetarians eating a wide variety of foods should therefore have no problem in obtaining enough B vitamins, although vegans (who do not eat dairy products) need to include some sort of B12 supplement in their diet.

Vitamin C is well known for helping to prevent infections and is firmly believed by many to assist in warding off, as well as curing, winter colds and 'flu. Eat foods rich in vitamin C with iron-rich foods, as it helps to increase the absorption of iron. Fresh fruit, leafy vegetables, tomatoes, peppers and potatoes are all good sources. Avoid drinking tea, coffee and certain soft drinks with foods that contain vitamin C, as the caffeine can actually decrease the amount of vitamin C your body subsequently absorbs. Since vitamin C is easily destroyed during cooking, only use a small amount of water when boiling vegetables to cook them as quickly as possible. This will minimize the risk of the vitamin leaching into the cooking water.

The other important vitamin for good health is vitamin D, which enables the body to absorb calcium, thus providing strong bones and teeth. Vitamin D is often known as the 'sunshine vitamin', as the body can manufacture its own supply from exposure to sunlight. Good food sources include eggs, cheese, margarine and butter.

Minerals

Minerals are another group of vital nutrients that are needed by the human body. Although only minute amounts are required, minerals need to be supplied on a regular basis. It makes sense to get to know which foods contain them, and make sure you are getting plenty of these in your diet. There should be no problem as long as you eat a wide variety of foods.

Calcium is found in milk, cheese, yogurt and other dairy products, leafy green vegetables, bread, nuts, seeds and dried fruits. Iron is found in beans, seeds, nuts, eggs, cocoa, chocolate, wholemeal bread, leafy green vegetables and dried fruits (especially apricots and figs). Other important minerals include magnesium, phosphorus, potassium and zinc.

THE VEGETARIAN SHOPPING BASKET

When shopping for vegetarian foods, make sure that you are not buying animal products unawares. Choose cheese that is made from vegetarian rennet; buy agar-agar or gelozone instead of gelatine; select a vegetarian suet instead of beef suet – no, you won't have to forego delicious dumplings!

Be aware of what you are spreading on your bread too. Some margarines are not suitable as they contain both fish oils and animal fats, so check that you are buying a brand made entirely of vegetable oil. Butter is perfect, unless, of course, you are a vegan.

The Vegetarian Store-cupboard

A well-stocked store-cupboard forms the backbone of any good cook's kitchen, and it is always useful to have plenty of basic foods ready to hand. Use the following information as a checklist when you need to replenish your stocks.

Flour

You will need to keep a selection of flours: plain and self-raising flour if you want to make your own bread, and wholemeal flour, either for using on its own or for combining with white flour for cakes and pastries. You may also like to keep some rice flour and cornflour for thickening sauces and to add to cakes, biscuits and puddings. Buckwheat, chick-pea and soya flours can also be bought. These are useful for pancakes and for combining with other flours to add different flavours and textures.

Grains

A good variety of grains is essential. For rice, choose from long-grain, basmati, Italian arborio for making risotto, short-grain for puddings, and wild rice to add flavour and interest. Look out for fragrant Thai rice, jasmine rice and combinations of different varieties to add colour and texture to your dishes. When choosing your rice, remember that brown rice is a much better source of vitamin B1 and fibre.

Other grains add variety to the diet. Try to include some barley (whole grain or pearl), millet, bulgar wheat, polenta (made from maize), oats (oatmeal, oatflakes or oatbran), semolina – including cous-cous (from which it is made), sago and tapioca.

Pasta

Pasta has become much more popular recently, and there are many types and shapes to choose from. Keep a good selection, and always make sure you have the basic lasagne sheets, tagliatelle or fettuccine (flat ribbons) and spaghetti. Try spinach- or tomato-flavoured varieties for a change, and sample some of the many fresh pastas now available. Better still, make your own – handrolling pasta, while undoubtedly time-consuming, can be very satisfying, but you can buy a special machine for rolling the dough and cutting certain shapes. You could also buy a wooden 'pasta tree' on which to hang the pasta to dry, in which case you might find you get enthusiastic help especially if you have small children!

Pulses

Pulses are very important in a vegetarian diet as they are a valuable source of protein, vitamins and minerals. Stock up on soya beans, haricot beans, red kidney beans, cannellini beans, chick-peas, all types of lentils, split peas and butter beans. Buy dried pulses for soaking and cooking yourself, or canned varieties for speed and convenience.

It is important to cook dried red and black kidney beans in plenty of vigorously boiling water for 15 minutes to destroy harmful toxins in the outer skin. Drain and rinse the beans, and then continue to simmer until the beans are tender. Soya beans should be boiled for 1 hour, as they contain a substance that inhibits protein absorption.

Spices and Herbs

A good selection of spices and herbs is important for adding variety and interest to your cooking – add to your range each time you try a new recipe. There are some good spice mixtures available – try Cajun, Chinese five-spice powder, Indonesian piri-piri and the different curry blends. Try grinding your own spices with a mortar and pestle, or in a coffee mill (wash well after using!), to make your own blends, or just experiment with those that you can buy. Although spices will keep well, don't leave them in the cupboard for too long, as they may lose some of their strength. Buy small amounts as you need them.

Fresh herbs are always preferable to dried, but it is essential to have dried ones in stock as a useful back-up. Keep the basics such as thyme, rosemary, bay leaves and some good Mediterranean mixtures for Italian and French cooking.

Chillies

These come both fresh and dried and in colours from green through yellow, orange and red to brown. The 'hotness' varies so use with caution, but as a guide the smaller they are the hotter they will be. The seeds are hottest and are usually discarded. When cutting chillies with bare hands do not touch your eyes: the juices will cause severe irritation.

Chilli powder should also be used sparingly. Check whether the powder is pure chilli or a chilli seasoning or blend, which should be milder. Chilli sauces are also used widely in oriental cookery, but again they vary in strength from hot to exceedingly hot, as well as in sweetness.

Nuts and Seeds

As well as adding protein, vitamins and useful fats to the diet, nuts and seeds add important flavour and texture to vegetarian meals. To bring out the flavour of nuts and seeds, grill or roast them until lightly browned.

Make sure that you keep a good supply of almonds, brazils, cashews, chestnuts (dried or canned), hazelnuts, peanuts, pecans, pistachios, pine kernels and walnuts. Coconut – either creamed or desiccated – is useful too.

For your seed collection, sesame, sunflower, pumpkin and poppy seeds are a good choice. Pumpkin seeds in particular are an excellent source of zinc.

Dried Fruits

Currants, raisins, sultanas, dates, apples, apricots, figs, pears, peaches, prunes, paw-paws, mangoes, figs, bananas and pineapples can all be purchased dried and can be used in lots of different recipes. When buying dried fruits, look for untreated varieties: for example, buy figs that have not been rolled in sugar, and choose unsulphured apricots, if they are available.

Though dried fruits are a healthier alternative to biscuits and sweets, they are still high in calories, being a natural source of sugar.

Oils and Fats

Oils are useful for adding subtle flavourings to foods, so it is a good idea to have a selection in your store-cupboard. Use a light olive oil for cooking and extra-virgin olive oil for salad dressings. Use sunflower oil as a good general-purpose oil and select one or two speciality oils to add character to different dishes. Sesame oil is wonderful in stir-fries; hazelnut and walnut oils are superb in salad dressings.

Oils and fats add flavour to foods, and contain the important fat-soluble vitamins A, D, E and K. Remember all fats and oils are high in calories, and that oils are higher in calories than butter or margarine – one tablespoon of oil contains 134 calories, whereas one tablespoon of butter or margarine contains 110 calories. When you are using oil in dressings or adding it to a wok or frying pan, it is a good idea to measure it – it's easy to use twice as much without realizing.

Vinegars

Choose three or four vinegars – red or white wine, cider, light malt, tarragon, sherry or balsamic vinegar, to name just a few. Each will add its own character to your recipes.

Mustards

Mustards are made from black, brown or white mustard seeds which are ground, mixed with spices and then, usually, mixed with vinegar.

Meaux mustard is made from mixed mustard seeds and has a grainy texture with a warm, spicy taste.

Dijon mustard, made from husked and ground mustard

seeds, is medium-hot and has a sharp flavour. Its versatility in salads and with barbecues makes it an ideal mustard for the vegetarian. It is made in Dijon, France, and only mustard made there can be labelled as such.

German mustard is mild sweet/sour and is best used in Scandinavian and German dishes.

Bottled Sauces

Soy sauce is widely used in all Eastern cookery and is made from fermented yellow soya beans mixed with wheat, salt, yeast and sugar. It comes in both light and dark varieties. Light soy sauce tends to be rather salty, whereas dark soy sauce tends to be sweeter and is more often used in dips and sauces.

Teriyaki sauce gives an authentic Japanese flavouring to stir-fries. Thick and dark brown, it contains soy sauce, vinegar, sesame oil and spices as main ingredients.

Black bean and yellow bean sauces add an instant authentic Chinese flavour to stir-fries. Black bean sauce is the stronger; the yellow bean variety is milder and is excellent with vegetables.

USEFUL EXTRAS

Tahini (sesame seed paste), yeast extract, sea salt, black and green peppercorns, tomato and garlic purées, vegetable stock cubes, dried yeast, gelozone or agar-agar are all useful store-cupboard additions.

THE VEGETARIAN FRIDGE AND FREEZER

Thankfully, food manufacturers have wised up to the fact that lots of us love to eat vegetarian food, so it is now possible to choose from a huge range of prepared meals from the chilled or frozen food cabinets. These are excellent standbys for when you want a meal in a hurry, and they add variety and choice to the diet. Pasta dishes, vegetable bakes and burgers, curries, flans and quiches are just some of the dishes to choose from.

Besides stocking a selection of ready-made meals, freeze other basics such as frozen pastries (shortcrust, filo or puff pastry); a selection of breads, such as pitta, French bread, rolls or part-baked bread; pre-cooked pasta dishes, pasta sauces, vegetable stock, breadcrumbs, home-made soups and sauces, flan cases, pancakes, pizza bases, and so on. All these will be useful when you are short of time.

THE SECRET OF SUCCESS

As with any cooking, the choice of ingredients is of paramount importance. If they are fresh and of good quality, you are well on your way to achieving delicious food. Not only will the flavours be better, but so will the colours, textures and nutritious value. Fresh fruit and vegetables lose their vitamin content very quickly if stored for too long, so buy from the freshest possible source, and use soon after buying.

Basic Recipes

Vegetarian stocks and sauces are invaluable for many recipes. Here are a few basics.

Fresh Vegetable Stock

This can be kept chilled for up to three days or frozen for up to three months. Salt is not added when cooking the stock: it is better to season it according to the dish in which it is to be used. Makes 1.5 litres/ 2½ pints.

250 g/9 oz shallots
1 large carrot, diced
1 celery stalk, chopped
½ fennel bulb
1 garlic clove
1 bay leaf
a few fresh parsley and tarragon sprigs
2 litres/3½ pints water
pepper

1 Put all the ingredients in a large saucepan and bring to the boil. Skim off the surface scum with a flat spoon and reduce to a gentle simmer. Partially cover and cook for 45 minutes. Leave to cool.

2 Line a sieve with clean muslin and put over a large jug or bowl. Pour the stock through the sieve. Discard the herbs and vegetables. Cover and store in small quantities in the refrigerator for up to three days.

Tahini Cream

Tahini is a paste made from sesame seeds. This nutty-flavoured sauce is good served with Falafel (see page 68) and other Middle Eastern dishes. Makes 150 ml/¼ pint.

3 tbsp tahini (sesame seed paste)
6 tbsp water
2 tsp lemon juice
1 garlic clove, crushed
salt and pepper

1 Blend together the tahini and water. Stir in the lemon juice and garlic. Season with salt and freshly ground black pepper.

Béchamel Sauce

This basic white sauce can be used in all kinds of dishes. Flavour it with grated cheese or chopped fresh herbs if you like. Makes 600 ml/1 pint.

600 ml/1 pint milk
4 cloves
1 bay leaf
pinch of freshly grated nutmeg
25 g/1 oz butter or vegetarian margarine
25 g/1 oz plain flour
salt and pepper

1 Put the milk in a saucepan and add the cloves, bay leaf and nutmeg. Gradually bring to the boil. Remove from the heat and leave for 15 minutes.

2 Melt the butter or margarine in another saucepan and stir in the flour to form a roux. Cook, stirring, for 1 minute.

3 Remove from the heat. Strain the milk and gradually blend into the roux.

4 Return to the heat and bring to the boil, stirring, until the sauce thickens. Season and add any flavourings.

Salads

*Salads are such a versatile way of eating, and the variety of ingredients
is so great, that they can be made to suit any occasion, from a light piquant
starter to a more substantial dish to serve as a main course, or a mixture
of exotic fruits for a delicious dessert.*

SALAD INGREDIENTS

A salad is the ideal emergency meal. It is quick to 'rustle up' and there are times when you might discover that you already have a really good combination of ingredients to hand when you need to present a meal-in-a-moment. A splash of culinary inspiration, and you will find you have prepared a fantastic salad that you had no idea was lurking in your kitchen!

Salads can be fruity, eggy, cheesy, made with grains or pulses, or just fresh green – all are highly nutritious. They are also generally low in calories if you go easy on the dressing, or use a fat-free dressing. It is easy to make a salad look attractive and appetizing, thus encouraging your family to eat fruit and vegetables. It is also often a welcome dish to serve alongside richer offerings.

Supermarkets now stock many unusual ingredients, which can add interest to an ordinary salad. Experiment with new

fruits and vegetables, buying them in small quantities to lend unusual flavours to salads made from cheaper ingredients. Always use the freshest ingredients to ensure a successful salad. Try to ensure that you buy fruit and vegetables at their peak and use them within a few days of buying.

Herbs
Every salad can be turned into something special with the addition of a few carefully chosen herbs to add flavour and a delicious aroma. The recipes in this book make liberal use of fresh herbs, adding a unique 'zip' to the food. Experiment with different varieties each time you make a salad or a dressing; try marjoram, thyme, chives, basil, mint, fennel and dill as well as the ubiquitous parsley. Basil goes especially well with tomatoes, and fennel or dill are particularly good with cucumber or beetroot salads.

Flowers
For an extra-special salad, add a few edible flowers, which look particularly colourful and attractive especially when mixed with a variety of salad leaves. Common sense is the best guide as to which flowers may be used whole and which should have the petals gently separated from the calyx. Borage, primroses, violas, pot marigolds, nasturtiums, violets, rock geraniums and rose petals are all suitable, imparting a sweetness and intense colour contrast to any green salad. Chive flowers have a good strong flavour – the pretty mauve flower heads should be separated into florets before sprinkling over the salad.

It is, of course, important that the flowers should look fresh and clean. If they need washing, be sure to handle with great care. Gently pat dry with paper towels and then store them in a rigid plastic container in the refrigerator until required.

It goes without saying that flowers which have been sprayed with insecticide should not be used.

Nuts
In addition to colour and flavour, salads need texture, which can be achieved by combining crunchy ingredients with softer fruits and vegetables. Nuts are particularly useful in this respect, contributing a pleasant crunchiness as well as

flavour. Many nuts taste even better if they are browned before use. These include almonds, hazelnuts, pine kernels and peanuts. To brown nuts, place them on a baking sheet and place in a hot oven for 5–10 minutes until golden brown. Pine kernels may also be browned by placing in a dry heavy-based frying pan and shaking over a high heat until golden.

Chicory This is available from autumn to spring and, with its slightly bitter flavour, makes an interesting addition to winter salads. Choose firm, tightly packed cones with yellow leaf tips. Avoid any with damaged leaves or leaf tips that are turning green as they will be rather too bitter. Red chicory is also available.

Chinese Leaves These are a most useful salad ingredient available in the autumn and winter months. Shred them fairly finely and use them as a base, adding bean-shoots and peppery leaves such as watercress or dandelion.

Cos Lettuce This is a superb variety used especially in Caesar salad. It has long, narrow, bright green leaves with a wonderfully crisp texture.

Endive A slightly bitter-tasting but attractive curly-leaved salad plant. There are two varieties: the curly endive (frisée) which has a mop head of light green frilly leaves and the Batavia endive (escarole) which has broader, smoother leaves. Before they mature, both varieties have their leaves tied together to blanch the centres, which produces tender, succulent leaves.

Feuille de Chêne This red-tinged, delicately flavoured lettuce is good when mixed with other leaves, both for the contrast in flavour and the contrast in colour.

Iceberg Lettuce This has pale green, densely packed leaves. It may appear expensive, but is in fact extremely good value when compared with other lettuces by weight. It has a fresh, crisp texture and keeps well in the refrigerator.

Lamb's Lettuce This is so called because its dark green leaves resemble a lamb's tongue. It is also known as corn salad and the French call it mâche. It is well worth looking out for when it is in season both for its flavour and its appearance.

Purslane This has fleshy stalks and rosettes of succulent green leaves which have a sharp, clean flavour.

Radicchio This is a variety of chicory originating in Italy. It looks rather like a small, tightly packed red lettuce. It is quite expensive but comparatively few leaves are needed, as it has a bitter flavour. The leaves are a deep purple colour with a white contrasting rib. They add character to any green salad.

Rocket The young green leaves of this plant have a distinctive warm peppery flavour and are delicious in green salads.

Round or Cabbage Lettuce This is the one most familiar to us all. Try to avoid the hothouse variety as the leaves are limp and floppy.

Salad leaves

Supermarkets now stock a wonderful variety of previously-hard-to-find salad leaves, so experiment with different types. The raw leaves from young leafy vegetables can also be used.

Watercress This has a fresh peppery taste which makes it a welcome addition to many salads. It is available throughout the year, though it is less good when flowering, or early in the season when the leaves are small.

PREPARING SALAD LEAVES

Whichever salad leaves you choose, they should be firm and crisp with no sign of browning or wilting. They should be handled with care because salad leaves bruise easily.

To prepare, pull off and discard all damaged outer leaves and wash the remaining leaves in cold salted water to remove any insects, then dry them thoroughly. This can be done either by patting the leaves dry with paper towels, spinning them in a salad spinner, or by placing them in a clean tea towel, gathering up the loose ends and swinging the tea towel around vigorously.

Dress the salad leaves just before serving. If you dress it any earlier the leaves will wilt.

DRESSINGS

All salads depend on being well dressed and so it is necessary to use the best ingredients. The principal ingredients in a salad dressing are oil and vinegar, with a variety of other flavourings that can be varied to suit the particular salad.

The choice of oil is particularly important. Oils are produced from various nuts, seeds and beans and each has its own flavour. Unrefined oils, although more expensive, are worth using for their superior taste.

Olive Oil is the best oil for most salad dressings. Choose the green-tinged, fruity oil labelled 'extra virgin' or 'first pressing'. It has a distinctive taste and aroma.

Sesame Oil has a strong nutty tang and is particularly good with oriental-type salads.

Sunflower and Safflower Oil are neutral-flavoured oils and can be mixed with olive oil or used alone to produce a lighter dressing. Mayonnaise made with a combination of one of these oils and olive oil has a lighter consistency than one made from olive oil only.

Walnut and Hazelnut Oil have the most wonderful flavour and aroma, and are usually mixed with olive oil in a French dressing. They are well worth their higher price and are especially good with slightly bitter salad plants such as chicory, radicchio or spinach.

A good dressing needs a touch of acidity. Good quality vinegars such as wine, cider, sherry or herb-flavoured vinegars are ideal, but malt vinegar is far too harsh and overpowers the subtle balance of the dressing. Lemon juice may be used as a dressing and is often preferable if the salad is fruit-based.

Balsamic Vinegar is dark and mellow with a sweet/sour flavour. It is expensive but you need only a few drops or at most a teaspoonful to give a wonderful taste. It is made in the area around Modena in Italy.

Cider Vinegar is reputed to contain many healthy properties and valuable nutrients. It has a light, subtle flavour redolent of the fruit from which it is made.

Flavoured Vinegars can be made from cider and wine vinegar. To do this, steep your chosen ingredient in a small bottle of vinegar for anything up to two weeks. Particularly good additions are basil, tarragon, garlic, thyme, mint or rosemary. Raspberry wine vinegar can be made by adding about twelve raspberries to a bottle of vinegar.

Sherry Vinegar has a rich mellow flavour which blends well with walnut and hazelnut oils, but is equally good by itself.

Wine Vinegar is the one most commonly used for French dressing; either red or white will do.

SALAD DRESSINGS

Make up a large bottle of your favourite dressing. Here are some recipes for you to try:

Sesame Dressing

A piquant dressing with a rich creamy texture.

2 tbsp tahini (sesame seed paste)
2 tbsp cider vinegar
2 tbsp medium sherry
2 tbsp sesame oil
1 tbsp soy sauce
1 garlic clove, crushed

1 Put the tahini in a bowl and gradually mix in the vinegar and sherry until smooth.

2 Add the remaining ingredients and mix together thoroughly.

Tomato Dressing

This completely fat-free dressing is ideal if you are counting calories.

125 ml/4 fl oz tomato juice
1 garlic clove, crushed
2 tbsp lemon juice
1 tbsp soy sauce
1 tsp clear honey
2 tbsp chopped chives
salt and pepper

Put all the ingredients into a screw-top jar and shake vigorously until well mixed.

Apple & Cider Vinegar Dressing

2 tbsp sunflower oil
2 tbsp concentrated apple juice
2 tbsp cider vinegar
1 tbsp Meaux mustard
1 garlic clove, crushed
salt and pepper

Put the oil, apple juice, vinegar, mustard, garlic and salt and pepper to taste in a screw-top jar and shake vigorously until well mixed.

Green Herb Dressing

A pale green dressing with a fresh flavour, ideal with cauliflower or broccoli.

15 g/^{1}/$_2$ oz parsley
15 g/^{1}/$_2$ oz mint
15 g/^{1}/$_2$ oz chives
1 garlic clove, crushed
150 ml/^{1}/$_4$ pint natural yogurt
salt and pepper

1 Remove the stalks from the parsley and mint and put the leaves in a blender or food processor with the chives, garlic and yogurt.

2 Add seasoning to taste. Blend until smooth, then store in the refrigerator until needed.

Wok Cookery

Wok cookery is an excellent technique for vegetarians as it enables you to serve up delicious dishes of crisp, tasty vegetables in minutes.

PREPARING FOOD FOR THE WOK

Ensure all ingredients are to hand before you start to cook, otherwise the first ingredients will be overcooked before the others are ready to add. Although oriental cooks use a variety of cleavers for chopping, a sharp kitchen knife will do just as well. All ingredients should be cut into uniform sizes with as many cut surfaces exposed as possible, hence the practice of cutting on the slant or diagonal, or into julienne strips or matchsticks.

Stir-frying

This is the most popular method of cooking in a wok. Once the food has been prepared and you are ready to begin, add the oil to the wok and heat it, swirling it round until it is really hot. If it is sufficiently hot the ingredients added should sizzle and begin to cook.

Most recipes begin by cooking the onions, garlic and ginger, because they flavour the oil. The heat may need to be lowered a little at first but must be increased again as the other ingredients are added. Gas probably gives the best results because of the speed of controlling the heat, and the fact that the curved base of the wok fits so well into the hob. Electric and solid fuel hobs are more efficient if you are using a flat-bottomed wok.

Always add the ingredients in the order they are listed in the recipe. While the food is cooking, keep stirring. When you add a sauce or liquid at the end of a recipe, first push the cooked food to the side of the wok so the sauce heats as quickly as possible, then toss the food back into the sauce over a high heat so that it boils and thickens the sauce. Serve the cooked food as soon as possible.

Deep-frying

A wok is usually used for deep-frying battered egg-and-crumbed morsels of food or food encased in pastry. The best oil to use is groundnut, which has a high smoke point and mild flavour, so it will neither burn nor impart taste to the food.

If you have a round-bottomed wok, use a metal wok stand to keep it stable during cooking. It is not necessary to preheat the wok. Simply add the oil (about 600 ml/1 pint should be sufficient) and heat to 180°C–190°C/350°F–375°F or until a cube of bread browns in 30 seconds.

The cooking time is determined by the size of the ingredients to be cooked, and it is essential that the oil is hot enough to seal the batter or pastry as quickly as possible without the food absorbing any more oil than necessary. When golden brown, remove with a slotted spoon and drain on paper towels. Serve at once to retain the food's crispness.

Steaming

To steam food you need a large wok and a bamboo steamer with a lid. The wok needs a little water in the bottom but it must not reach the base of the bamboo steamer when it is in position: stand the steamer on a trivet. The steamer has several layers, which can be stacked on top of each other. This means more than one type of food can be cooked at the same time. Put the food on a plate that will just fit into the steamer and place it carefully in one of the layers. Add seasoning, herbs and flavourings, cover with the lid and steam until tender. Make sure the wok does not boil dry by adding extra water when necessary.

If you don't have a bamboo steamer, you can still steam food in the wok. Simply put a plate on a metal or wooden trivet in the wok, pour in enough water to come just below the plate and cover with a lid.

Braising/Simmering

The wok can also be used as a saucepan and is excellent for making stir-fry soups, for example. Just stir-fry the ingredients in a little oil, add the liquid seasonings and simmer either uncovered or with a lid. With this type of soup the vegetables should still have a good 'bite' to them, so the cooking time is a lot less than that of traditional soups.

Pan-frying and braising are speeded up using a wok because of the improved heat distribution. Simply fry the ingredients quickly, then add the stock or sauce, cover and simmer gently until tender. Sometimes it is better not to cover the wok so that the cooking liquid is reduced, intensifying the flavours even more. Whichever method is used, stir occasionally to prevent any possibility of sticking.

Vegetarian Barbecues

*There are so many tasty and nutritious vegetarian dishes that can be cooked over hot coals
– after all, barbecueing is just an alternative method of cooking by direct heat.*

PLANNING YOUR BARBECUE

Barbecues always take longer to get going than you expect, so allow plenty of time. Don't be tempted to start cooking too soon, or the coals will not be ready. The flames should have died down and the coals reduced to a steady glow before you begin.

Don't attempt to cook for a large party on a small barbecue, as it could take hours to feed everyone! In this situation, it is better to cook most of the food in the kitchen, and either provide only a few barbecued items, or use the barbecue to finish partly-cooked foods. Vegetarian sausages and burgers are ideal, as they cook quickly and in large quantities.

ADVANCE PREPARATIONS

Many foods for barbecuing will benefit from being marinated, especially dishes using tofu or Quorn, which absorb the flavour of the marinade. You can buy tofu in four varieties – smoked, firm, soft or silken; use smoked or firm for kebabs, soft for adding to burgers, and silken for adding to sauces and dips.

Have your kebabs ready-threaded for quick cooking; if possible, choose flat metal skewers so that the food does not slide as the kebabs are turned. Alternatively, use bamboo sticks, but soak them in water beforehand so that they do not burn over the hot coals and ruin the food.

Control the heat by adjusting the distance of the food from the coals, or by altering the controls on a gas barbecue. Ideally, food should not be cooked too quickly, or it will blacken and char on the outside before the middle is cooked – it needs time for the distinctive barbecued taste to be imparted.

COOKING TIPS

First and foremost, treat food for barbecuing with care – it should be kept chilled in the refrigerator or in a cool box, complete with ice packs, until ready to cook.

Light the barbecue in plenty of time, remembering that you will need about 45 minutes for charcoal to heat and about 10–15 minutes for a gas barbecue to become hot enough. Food cooks best over glowing embers, not smoking fuel, so avoid putting the food over the hot coals until the smoking has subsided. Oil the barbecue rack lightly before adding the food, to help to prevent it from sticking, and oil the skewers, tongs and barbecue fork for the same reason.

Throw some fresh herbs on to the coals – they smell wonderful as they burn, and will add extra flavour to your food. Woody herbs burn slowly, so they are good choices.

COOKING VEGETABLES

For kebabs, choose a mixture of vegetables that will all cook at the same rate, and cut into even-sized chunks. Choose from aubergines, tomatoes, sliced corn-on-the-cob or baby corn cobs, mushrooms and courgettes. New potatoes, onions, carrots, parsnips and Jerusalem artichokes can also be barbecued, but will need pre-cooking first.

If you are going to serve jacket potatoes, cook them first too – either conventionally or in a microwave. Wrap in foil and keep warm to one side of the barbecue, ready for filling. Or finish cooking potatoes directly on the grid over the coals, barbecueing them until the skins are crisp and brown.

Vegetables can be cooked in foil parcels as well as on kebab skewers. Slice them roughly, sprinkle with olive oil, herbs and seasonings and wrap tightly. Cook until tender.

Soups & Starters

Soup is simple to make but produces tasty results. A wide variety of soups can be made with vegetables – they can be rich and creamy, thick and chunky, light and delicate, and hot or chilled. The secret of a good soup lies in using a well-flavoured stock as the base. Although there are some excellent vegetable stock cubes available, a homemade stock (see page 14) gives the edge to any soup. A wide range of ingredients can be used in addition to vegetables – try using pulses, grains, noodles, vegetarian cheese and yogurt.

With so many fresh ingredients available, it is easy to create delicious starters that are the perfect introduction to a vegetarian meal. The ideas in this chapter are an inspiration to cook and a treat to eat, and they give an edge to the appetite that makes the main course even more enjoyable. A balance of flavours, colours and textures will offer variety and contrast.

Red Pepper & Chilli Soup

This soup has a real Mediterranean flavour, using sweet red peppers, tomato, chilli and basil. It is great served with a warm olive bread.

Serves 4
225 g/8 oz red peppers, seeded and sliced
1 onion, sliced
2 garlic cloves, crushed
1 green chilli, chopped
300 ml/½ pint passata
600 ml/1 pint vegetable stock
2 tbsp chopped basil
fresh basil sprigs, to garnish

1 Put the peppers in a large saucepan with the onion, garlic and chilli. Add the passata and stock and bring to the boil, stirring well.

2 Reduce the heat to a simmer and cook for 20 minutes or until the peppers have softened. Drain, reserving the liquid and vegetables separately.

3 Sieve the vegetables by pressing through a sieve with the back of a spoon, or blend in a food processor until smooth.

4 Return the vegetable purée to a clean saucepan with the reserved cooking liquid. Add the basil and heat through until hot. Garnish and serve.

COOK'S VARIATION

This soup is also delicious served cold with 150 ml/¼ pint of natural yogurt swirled into it.

Mixed Bean Soup

This is a really hearty soup, filled with colour, flavour and goodness,
which may be adapted to any vegetables that you have to hand.

Serves 4
1 tbsp vegetable oil
1 red onion, halved and sliced
100 g/3¹/₂ oz potato, diced
1 carrot, diced
1 leek, sliced
1 green chilli, sliced
3 garlic cloves, crushed
1 tsp ground coriander
1 tsp chilli powder
1 litre/2 pints vegetable stock
450 g/1 lb mixed canned beans, such as red kidney, borlotti, black eye or flageolet, drained
salt and pepper
2 tbsp chopped coriander, to garnish

1 Heat the oil in a large saucepan and add the onion, potato, carrot and leek. Sauté for 2 minutes, stirring, until slightly softened. Add the chilli and garlic and cook for a further 1 minute.

2 Stir in the ground coriander, chilli powder and the stock. Bring to the boil, reduce the heat and cook for 20 minutes or until the vegetables are tender.

3 Stir in the beans, season well and cook for a further 10 minutes. Garnish with chopped coriander and serve.

COOK'S TIP

Serve this soup with slices of warm corn bread or a cheese loaf.

Noodle, Mushroom & Ginger Soup

Thai soups are very quickly and easily put together, and are cooked
so that each ingredient can still be tasted in the finished dish.

Serves 4

15 g/¹/₂ oz dried
Chinese mushrooms
or 125 g/4¹/₂ oz field
or chestnut mushrooms

1 litre/1³/₄ pints hot Fresh Vegetable Stock
(see page 14)

125 g/4¹/₂ oz thread egg noodles

2 tsp sunflower oil

3 garlic cloves, crushed

2.5 cm/1 inch piece ginger,
shredded finely

¹/₂ tsp mushroom ketchup

1 tsp light soy sauce

125 g/4¹/₂ oz beansprouts

fresh coriander leaves,
to garnish

1 Soak the dried Chinese
mushrooms, if using, in 300 ml/¹/₂
pint of the hot vegetable stock for at
least 30 minutes. Remove the stalks
and discard, then slice the
mushrooms. Reserve the stock.

2 Cook the noodles in a saucepan of
boiling water for 2–3 minutes. Drain,
rinse and drain again. Set aside until
required.

3 Heat the oil over a high heat in a
wok or large, heavy frying pan. Add the
garlic and ginger, stirring. Add the
mushrooms and cook over a high heat
for 2 minutes, stirring well.

4 Add the remaining vegetable stock
with the reserved hot stock and bring
to the boil. Add the mushroom
ketchup and soy sauce.

5 Stir in the beansprouts and cook
until tender.

6 Pour the soup over the noodles,
garnish and serve.

COOK'S TIP

Dried Chinese mushrooms are available
from oriental stores.

Jerusalem Artichoke Soup

Jerusalem artichokes belong to the tuber family. They are native
to North America, but are also grown in Europe. They have a delicious nutty flavour
which combines well with the orange in this soup.

Serves 4
650 g/1¹/₂ lb Jerusalem artichokes
5 tbsp orange juice
25 g/1 oz butter
1 leek, chopped
1 garlic clove, crushed
300 ml/¹/₂ pint vegetable stock
150 ml/¹/₄ pint milk
2 tbsp chopped coriander
150 ml/¹/₄ pint natural yogurt
grated orange rind, to garnish

1 Rinse the Jerusalem artichokes
and place in a large saucepan with 2
tablespoons of the orange juice and
enough water to cover. Bring to the
boil, reduce the heat and cook for 20
minutes or until the artichokes are
tender. Drain the artichokes, reserving
450 ml/³/₄ pint of the cooking liquid.
Leave the artichokes to cool.

2 Peel the artichokes and mash the
flesh with a potato masher.

3 Melt the butter in a large saucepan
and sauté the leek and garlic for
2–3 minutes, stirring until the leek
softens.

4 Stir in the artichoke flesh, the
reserved cooking water, the stock,
milk and remaining orange juice.
Bring the soup to the boil, reduce the
heat and simmer for 2–3 minutes.

5 Reserving a few pieces of leek,
transfer the remainder of the soup to
a food processor and blend for 1
minute until smooth.

6 Return the soup to a clean saucepan
and stir in the reserved leeks,
coriander and yogurt.

7 Transfer to individual soup bowls,
garnish with orange rind and serve.

COOK'S VARIATION

If Jerusalem artichokes are unavailable,
you could use
sweet potatoes instead.

Broad Bean & Mint Soup

Fresh broad beans are best for this recipe, but if they are unavailable, use frozen beans instead. They combine well with the fresh flavour of mint.

Serves 4
2 tbsp olive oil
1 red onion, chopped
2 garlic cloves, crushed
2 potatoes, diced
450 g/1 lb broad beans, thawed if frozen
850 ml/1½ pints vegetable stock
2 tbsp freshly chopped mint
salt and pepper
fresh mint sprigs and yogurt, to garnish

1 Heat the oil in a large saucepan and sauté the onion and garlic for 2–3 minutes until softened.

2 Add the potatoes and cook for 5 minutes, stirring well. Stir in the beans and the stock, cover and simmer for 30 minutes or until the beans and potatoes are tender.

3 Reserving a few vegetables, place the remainder of the soup in a food processor or blender and purée until smooth.

4 Return the soup to a clean saucepan and add the reserved vegetables and mint. Serve garnished with swirls of yogurt and sprigs of fresh mint.

COOK'S VARIATION

Use fresh coriander and ½ tsp ground cumin as flavourings in the soup, if you prefer.

Gardener's Broth

This thick, hearty soup uses a variety of green vegetables with a flavouring
of ground coriander. A finishing touch of thinly sliced leeks adds texture.

Serves 4
40 g/1½ oz butter or vegetarian margarine
1 onion, chopped
1–2 garlic cloves, crushed
1 large leek
225 g/8 oz Brussels sprouts
125 g/4½ oz French or runner beans
1.2 litres/2 pints Fresh Vegetable Stock (see page 14)
125 g/4½ oz frozen peas
1 tbsp lemon juice
½ tsp ground coriander
4 tbsp double cream
salt and pepper

MELBA TOAST

4–6 slices white bread

1 Melt the butter or vegetarian margarine in a saucepan, add the onion and garlic and fry very gently, stirring occasionally, until they begin to soften but not colour.

2 Slice the white part of the leek very thinly and reserve; slice the remaining leeks. Slice the Brussels sprouts and thinly slice the beans.

3 Add the green part of the leeks, the Brussels sprouts and beans to the saucepan. Add the stock and bring to the boil. Simmer for 10 minutes.

4 Add the frozen peas, seasoning, lemon juice and ground coriander and simmer for 10–15 minutes or until the vegetables are tender.

5 Cool the soup a little, then press through a sieve or blend in a food processor or blender until smooth. Pour into a clean pan.

6 Add the reserved slices of leek to the soup, bring back to the boil and simmer for about 5 minutes until the leeks are tender. Adjust the seasoning according to taste, stir in the cream and reheat gently.

7 To make the melba toast, toast the bread on both sides under a preheated grill. Cut horizontally through the slices then toast the uncooked sides until they curl up. Serve immediately with the soup.

Gazpacho

This Spanish soup is full of chopped and grated vegetables with a puréed tomato base.
Serve with extra chopped vegetables and croûtons.

Serves 4

$^1/_2$ small cucumber

$^1/_2$ small green pepper,
chopped very finely

500 g/1 lb 2 oz ripe tomatoes, peeled or
400 g/14 oz can chopped tomatoes

$^1/_2$ onion, chopped coarsely

2–3 garlic cloves, crushed

3 tbsp olive oil

2 tbsp white wine vinegar

1–2 tbsp lemon or lime juice

2 tbsp tomato purée

425 ml/$^3/_4$ pint
tomato juice

salt and pepper

TO SERVE

chopped green pepper

thinly sliced onion rings

garlic croûtons

1 Coarsely grate the cucumber into a bowl and add the chopped green pepper, mixing well.

2 Blend the tomatoes, onion and garlic in a food processor or blender, then add the oil, vinegar, lemon or lime juice and tomato purée and blend until smooth. Alternatively, finely chop the tomatoes and finely grate the onion, then mix both with the garlic, oil, vinegar, lemon or lime juice and tomato purée.

3 Add the tomato mixture to the cucumber and green pepper mixture and combine.

4 Add the tomato juice and mix again.

5 Season to taste, cover the bowl with cling film and chill thoroughly for at least 6 hours, but preferably longer for the flavours to combine.

6 Prepare the side dishes of green pepper, onion rings and garlic croûtons to serve and arrange in individual serving bowls.

7 Ladle the soup into bowls, preferably from a soup tureen set on the table with the side dishes around it. Hand the dishes around to allow the guests to help themselves.

Beetroot Soup

Here are two variations using the same vegetable: a creamy soup made
with puréed cooked beetroot; and a traditional clear soup, Bortsch.

Serves 4-6
BORTSCH

500 g/1 lb 2 oz raw beetroot,
peeled and grated

2 carrots, chopped finely

1 large onion, chopped finely

1 garlic clove, crushed

1 bouquet garni

1.2 litres/2 pints Fresh
Vegetable Stock (see page 14)

2-3 tsp lemon juice

salt and pepper

150 ml/^{1}/$_4$ pint soured
cream, to serve

CREAMED BEETROOT SOUP

60 g/2 oz/^{1}/$_4$ cup butter or vegetarian
margarine

2 large onions, chopped finely

1-2 carrots, chopped

2 celery sticks, chopped

500 g/1 lb 2 oz cooked beetroot, diced

1-2 tbsp lemon juice

850 ml/1^1/$_2$ pints Fresh Vegetable Stock
(see page 14)

300 ml/^{1}/$_2$ pint milk

salt and pepper

TO SERVE

grated cooked beetroot or 6 tbsp soured
or double cream, lightly whipped

1 To make bortsch, place the beetroot,
carrots, onion, garlic, bouquet garni,
stock, lemon juice and seasoning in a
saucepan. Bring to the boil, cover and
simmer for 45 minutes.

2 Press the soup through a fine sieve
or a sieve lined with muslin, then
pour into a clean pan. Adjust the
seasoning and add extra lemon juice if
necessary. Bring to the boil and
simmer for 1–2 minutes. Serve with a
spoonful of soured cream swirled
through.

3 To make creamed beetroot soup,
melt the butter or margarine in a pan
and fry the onions, carrots and celery
until just beginning to colour.

4 Add the beetroot, 1 tablespoon of
lemon juice, the stock and seasoning
and bring to the boil. Cover and
simmer for 30 minutes until tender.

5 Cool slightly, then press through a
sieve or blend in a food processor or
blender. Pour into a clean pan, add the
milk and bring to the boil. Adjust the
seasoning and add extra lemon juice if
necessary. Serve.

Dahl Soup

Dahl is a name given to a delicious Indian lentil dish.
This soup is a variation of the theme – it is made with red lentils
and spiced with curry powder.

Serves 4

25 g/1 oz butter
2 garlic cloves, crushed
1 onion, chopped
$^1/_2$ tsp turmeric
1 tsp garam masala
$^1/_4$ tsp chilli powder
1 tsp ground cumin
1 kg/2 lb 4 oz canned, chopped tomatoes, drained
175 g/6 oz red lentils
2 tsp lemon juice
600 ml/1 pint vegetable stock
300 ml/$^1/_2$ pint coconut milk
chopped coriander and lemon slices, to garnish
naan bread, to serve

1 Melt the butter in a large saucepan and sauté the garlic and onion for 2–3 minutes, stirring. Add the spices and cook for a further 30 seconds.

2 Stir in the tomatoes, lentils, lemon juice, stock and coconut milk and bring to the boil. Reduce the heat and simmer for 25–30 minutes until the lentils are tender and cooked.

3 Season and spoon the soup into a warm tureen. Garnish and serve with warm naan bread.

COOK'S TIP

Add small quantities of hot water to the pan whilst the lentils are cooking if they begin to absorb too much of the liquid.

Vichyssoise

This is a classic creamy soup made from potatoes and leeks.
To achieve the delicate pale colour, be sure to use only the white parts of the leeks.

Serves 4–6
3 large leeks
45 g/1½ oz butter or vegetarian margarine
1 onion, sliced thinly
500 g/1 lb 2 oz potatoes, chopped
850 ml/1½ pints Fresh Vegetable Stock (see page 14)
2 tsp lemon juice
pinch of ground nutmeg
¼ tsp ground coriander
1 bay leaf
1 egg yolk
150 ml/¼ pint single cream
salt and white pepper
snipped chives, to garnish

1 Trim the leeks and remove most of the green part (it can be served as a vegetable). Slice the white part of the leeks very finely.

2 Melt the butter or margarine in a saucepan and gently fry the leeks and onion for about 5 minutes without browning, stirring from time to time.

3 Add the potatoes, stock, lemon juice, salt and white pepper to taste, ground nutmeg, ground coriander and bay leaf to the pan and bring to the boil. Cover and simmer for about 30 minutes or until all of the vegetables are very soft.

4 Leave the soup to cool a little, then discard the bay leaf. Press the soup through a sieve or blend in a food processor or blender until smooth.

Pour the soup into a clean saucepan.

5 Blend the egg yolk into the cream. Add a little of the soup to the egg and cream mixture and then whisk it all back into the soup and reheat gently without boiling. Add a little more salt and white pepper to taste, if necessary. Cool and chill thoroughly before serving.

6 Serve the soup sprinkled with freshly snipped chives.

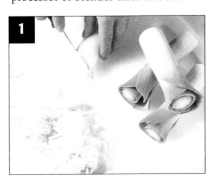

Curried Parsnip Soup

Parsnips make a delicious soup as they have a slightly sweet flavour. In this recipe, spices are added to complement this sweetness and a dash of lemon juice adds tartness.

Serves 4
1 tbsp vegetable oil
1 tbsp butter
1 red onion, chopped
3 parsnips, chopped
2 garlic cloves, crushed
2 tsp garam masala
1/2 tsp chilli powder
1 tbsp plain flour
850 ml/1 1/2 pints vegetable stock
grated rind and juice of 1 lemon
salt and pepper
lemon zest, to garnish

1 Heat the oil and butter in a large saucepan until the butter has melted.

2 Add the onion, parsnips and garlic and sauté for 5–7 minutes, stirring, until the vegetables have softened.

3 Add the garam masala and chilli powder and cook for 30 seconds, stirring well.

4 Sprinkle in the flour, mixing well and cook for a further 30 seconds.

5 Stir in the stock, lemon rind and juice and bring to the boil. Reduce the heat and simmer for 20 minutes or until the parsnips are tender.

6 Remove some of the vegetable pieces with a slotted spoon and reserve until required. Blend the remaining soup and vegetables in a food processor for 1 minute or until smooth.

7 Return the soup to a clean saucepan and stir in the reserved vegetables. Heat the soup through for 2 minutes.

8 Transfer to soup bowls, garnish with grated lemon zest and serve.

COOK'S VARIATION

Use 1 medium orange instead of the lemon if preferred and garnish with grated orange zest.

Avocado & Vegetable Soup

Avocado has a rich flavour and colour which makes a creamy flavoured soup.
It is best served chilled, but may be eaten warm as well.

Serves 4
1 large, ripe avocado
2 tbsp lemon juice
1 tbsp vegetable oil
50 g/1^3/$_4$ oz canned sweetcorn, drained
2 tomatoes, peeled and seeded
1 garlic clove, crushed
1 leek, chopped
1 red chilli, chopped
425 ml/^{3}/$_4$ pint vegetable stock
150 ml/^{1}/$_4$ pint milk
shredded leeks, to garnish

1 Peel and mash the avocado with a fork, stir in the lemon juice and reserve until required.

2 Heat the oil in a pan and sauté the sweetcorn, tomatoes, garlic, leek and chilli for 2–3 minutes until softened.

3 Put half of the vegetable mixture in a food processor or blender with the avocado and blend until smooth. Transfer to a clean saucepan.

4 Add the stock and milk and reserved vegetables and cook gently for 3–4 minutes until hot. Garnish with shredded leeks and serve.

COOK'S TIP

If serving chilled, transfer from the food processor to a bowl, stir in the stock and milk, cover and chill in the refrigerator for at least 4 hours.

Soft Cheese & Fresh Herb Soup

Make the most of home-grown herbs to create this wonderfully
creamy soup with its marvellous garden-fresh fragrance.

Serves 4
25 g/1 oz butter
or vegetarian margarine
2 onions, chopped
850 ml/1¹/₂ pints Fresh Vegetable Stock (see page 14)
25 g/1 oz coarsely chopped mixed fresh herbs, such as parsley, chives, thyme, basil and oregano
200 g/7 oz full-fat soft cheese
1 tbsp cornflour
1 tbsp milk
snipped fresh chives, to garnish

1 Melt the butter or margarine in a large saucepan and add the onions. Fry for 2 minutes, then cover and reduce the heat to low. Allow the onions to cook gently for 5 minutes, then remove the lid.

2 Add the stock and herbs to the saucepan. Bring to the boil, then reduce the heat. Cover and simmer gently for 20 minutes.

3 Remove the saucepan from the heat. Blend the soup in a food processor or blender for about 15 seconds, until smooth. Alternatively, press it through a sieve. Return the soup to the saucepan.

4 Spoon the soft cheese into the soup and whisk until fully incorporated.

5 Mix the cornflour with the milk, then stir into the soup and heat,

stirring constantly, until thickened and smooth. Pour the soup into 4 warmed bowls. Garnish with snipped chives and serve at once.

COOK'S TIP

Cheese is a good source of vitamins.

Celery, Stilton & Walnut Soup

This is a classic combination of ingredients all brought
together in a delicious, creamy soup.

Serves 4
50 g/1³/₄ oz butter
2 shallots, chopped
3 celery sticks, chopped
1 garlic clove, crushed
2 tbsp plain flour
600 ml/1 pint vegetable stock
300 ml/¹/₂ pint milk
150 g/5¹/₂ oz blue Stilton cheese, crumbled, plus extra to garnish
2 tbsp walnut halves, roughly chopped
150 ml/¹/₄ pint natural yogurt
salt and pepper
chopped celery leaves, to garnish

1 Melt the butter in a large saucepan
and sauté the shallots, celery and
garlic for 2–3 minutes, stirring, until
softened.

2 Add the flour and cook for
30 seconds.

3 Gradually stir in the stock and milk
and bring to the boil.

4 Reduce the heat to a gentle simmer
and add the cheese and walnuts.
Cover and leave to simmer for
20 minutes.

5 Stir in the yogurt and heat for a
further 2 minutes without boiling.

6 Transfer to a warm soup tureen or
individual serving bowls, garnish with
chopped celery leaves and extra
crumbled blue Stilton cheese and
serve at once.

COOK'S TIP

As well as adding protein, vitamins and
useful fats to the diet, nuts add
important flavour and texture to
vegetarian meals.

COOK'S VARIATION

Use an alternative blue cheese, such as
Dolcelatte or Gorgonzola, if preferred or
a strong vegetarian Cheddar cheese,
grated.

Pumpkin Soup

This is an American classic that has now become popular worldwide.
When pumpkin is out of season use butternut squash instead.

Serves 4–6
about 1 kg/2 lb 4 oz pumpkin
45 g/1$^{1}/_{2}$ oz butter or vegetarian margarine
1 onion, sliced thinly
1 garlic clove, crushed
850 ml/1$^{1}/_{2}$ pints Fresh Vegetable Stock (see page 14)
$^{1}/_{2}$ tsp ground ginger
1 tbsp lemon juice
3–4 thinly pared strips of orange rind (optional)
1–2 bay leaves or 1 bouquet garni
300 ml/$^{1}/_{2}$ pint milk
salt and pepper

TO GARNISH

4–6 tablespoons single or double cream, natural yogurt or fromage frais
snipped fresh chives

1 Peel the pumpkin, remove the seeds and then cut the flesh into 2.5 cm/1 inch cubes.

2 Melt the butter or margarine in a large saucepan, add the onion and garlic and fry gently until soft but not coloured.

3 Add the pumpkin and toss with the onion for 1–2 minutes.

4 Add the stock and bring to the boil. Add the seasoning, ginger, lemon juice, strips of orange rind, if using, and bay leaves or bouquet garni. Cover and simmer gently for about 20 minutes or until the pumpkin is very tender.

5 Discard the orange rind, if using, and the bay leaves or bouquet garni. Cool the soup a little and then press through a sieve or blend in a food processor or blender until smooth.

Pour the soup into a clean saucepan.

6 Add the milk and reheat gently. Adjust the seasoning to taste. Garnish with a swirl of cream, natural yogurt or fromage frais and snipped chives, and serve immediately.

Hot & Sour Soup

A very traditional staple of the Thai national diet, this soup is sold on street corners,
at food bars and by mobile vendors all over the country.

Serves 4

1 tbsp sunflower oil

225 g/8 oz smoked tofu,
sliced

90 g/3 oz shiitake
mushrooms, sliced

2 tbsp chopped fresh coriander

125 g/4½ oz watercress

1 red chilli, sliced finely, to garnish

STOCK

1 tbsp tamarind pulp

2 dried red chillies, chopped

2 kaffir lime leaves, torn in half

2.5 cm/1 inch piece ginger root,
chopped

5 cm/2 inch piece galangal, chopped

1 stalk lemon grass, chopped

1 onion, quartered

1 litre/1¾ pints
cold water

1 Put all the ingredients for the
stock into a saucepan and bring to the
boil. Simmer for 5 minutes. Remove
from the heat and strain, reserving
the stock.

2 Heat the oil in a wok or large, heavy
frying pan and cook the tofu over a
high heat for about 2 minutes, stirring
constantly. Pour in the strained stock.

3 Add the mushrooms and coriander
and boil for 3 minutes. Add the
watercress and boil for 1 minute.
Serve at once, garnished with chilli
slices, if wished.

Spanish Tomato Soup

This Mediterranean tomato soup is thickened with bread,
as is traditional in some parts of Spain.

Serves 4
4 tbsp olive oil
1 onion, chopped
3 garlic cloves, crushed
1 green pepper, chopped
$1/2$ tsp chilli powder
450 g/1 l tomatoes, chopped
225 g/8 oz French or Italian bread, cubed
1 litre/2 pints vegetable stock

GARLIC BREAD

4 slices ciabatta or French bread
4 tbsp olive oil
2 garlic cloves, crushed
25 g/1 oz grated vegetarian Cheddar
chilli powder, to garnish

1 Heat the oil in a large frying pan and sauté the onion, garlic and pepper for 2–3 minutes or until the onion has softened.

2 Add the chilli powder and tomatoes and cook over a medium heat until the mixture has thickened.

3 Stir in the bread and stock and cook for 10–15 minutes until the soup is thick and fairly smooth.

4 To make the garlic bread, toast the bread slices under a medium grill. Drizzle the oil over the top of the bread, rub with the garlic, sprinkle with the cheese and return to the grill for 2–3 minutes until the cheese has melted. Sprinkle with chilli powder and serve with the soup.

Fiery Salsa with Tortilla Chips

Make this Mexican-style salsa to perk up jaded palates.
Its lively flavours really get the tastebuds going.

Serves 6
2 small red chillies
1 tbsp lime or lemon juice
2 large ripe avocados
5 cm/2 inch piece cucumber
2 tomatoes, peeled
1 small garlic clove, crushed
few drops of Tabasco sauce
salt and pepper
lime or lemon slices, to garnish
tortilla chips, to serve

1 Remove and discard the stem and seeds from 1 chilli. Chop very finely and place in a mixing bowl. To make a chilli 'flower' for garnish, slice the remaining chilli from the stem to the tip several times without removing the stem. Place in a bowl of cold water, so that the 'petals' open out.

2 Add the lime or lemon juice to the mixing bowl. Halve, stone and peel the avocados. Add to the mixing bowl and mash with a fork. (The lime or lemon juice prevents the avocado from turning brown.)

3 Chop the cucumber and tomatoes finely and add to the avocado mixture with the crushed garlic.

4 Season the dip to taste with Tabasco sauce, salt and pepper.

5 Transfer the dip to a serving bowl. Garnish with slices of lime or lemon and the chilli flower. Put the bowl on a large plate, surround with tortilla chips and serve.

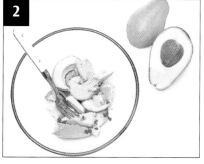

Hummus & Garlic Toasts

Hummus is a real favourite spread on these garlic toasts for a
delicious starter or as part of a light lunch.

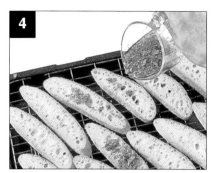

Serves 4
HUMMUS
400 g/14 oz can chick-peas
juice and rind of 1 large lemon
6 tbsp tahini (sesame seed paste)
2 tbsp olive oil
2 garlic cloves, crushed
salt and pepper
chopped fresh coriander and black olives, to garnish
TOASTS
1 ciabatta loaf, sliced
2 garlic cloves, crushed
1 tbsp chopped fresh coriander
4 tbsp olive oil

1 To make the hummus, firstly drain the chick-peas, reserving a little of the liquid. Put the chick-peas and liquid in a food processor and blend, gradually adding the reserved liquid and lemon juice. Blend well after each addition until smooth.

2 Stir in the tahini and all but 1 teaspoon of the olive oil. Add the garlic, season to taste and blend again until smooth. Spoon the hummus into a serving dish. Drizzle the remaining olive oil over the top, garnish with chopped coriander and olives and top with the lemon rind. Chill whilst preparing the toasts.

3 Lay the slices of ciabatta on a grill rack in a single layer.

4 Mix the garlic, coriander and olive oil together and drizzle over the bread

slices. Cook under a hot grill for 2–3 minutes until golden brown, turning once. Serve hot with the hummus.

COOK'S TIP

Make the hummus 1 day in advance, and chill, covered, in the refrigerator until required. Garnish and serve.

Vegetable Fritters with Sweet & Sour Sauce

These mixed vegetable fritters are coated in a light batter and deep fried until golden for a deliciously crisp coating. They are ideal with the sweet and sour dipping sauce.

Serves 4
100 g/3^1/$_2$ oz wholemeal flour
pinch of salt
pinch of cayenne pepper
4 tsp olive oil
12 tbsp cold water
100 g/3^1/$_2$ oz broccoli florets
100 g/3^1/$_2$ oz cauliflower florets
50 g/1^3/$_4$ oz mangetout
1 large carrot, cut into batons
1 red pepper, sliced
2 egg whites, beaten
oil, for deep-frying
SAUCE
150 ml/^{1}/$_4$ pint pineapple juice
150 ml/^{1}/$_4$ pint vegetable stock
2 tbsp wine vinegar
2 tbsp light brown sugar
2 tsp cornflour
2 spring onions, chopped

1 Sieve the flour and salt into a mixing bowl and add the cayenne pepper. Make a well in the centre and gradually beat in the oil and cold water to make a smooth batter.

2 Cook the vegetables in boiling water for 5 minutes and drain well.

3 Whisk the egg whites until peaking and fold them into the flour batter.

4 Dip the vegetables into the batter, turning to coat well. Drain off any excess batter. Heat the oil for deep-frying in a deep fat fryer to 180°C/350°F or until a cube of bread browns in 30 seconds. Fry the vegetables for

1–2 minutes, in batches, until golden. Remove from the oil with a slotted spoon and drain on kitchen paper.

5 Place all of the sauce ingredients in a pan and bring to the boil, stirring, until thickened and clear. Serve with the vegetable fritters.

COOK'S VARIATION

Use any variety of vegetables that you have to hand for the fritters, such as cubes of potato or sweet potato, or green beans.

Cheese, Garlic & Herb Pâté

This wonderful soft cheese pâté is fragrant with the aroma of fresh herbs and garlic.
Serve with triangles of Melba toast to make the perfect starter.

Serves 4
15 g/¹/₂ oz butter
1 garlic clove, crushed
3 spring onions, chopped finely
125 g/4¹/₂ oz full-fat soft cheese
2 tbsp chopped mixed fresh herbs, such as parsley, chives, marjoram, oregano and basil
175 g/6 oz mature Cheddar, grated finely
4–6 slices of white bread from a medium-cut sliced loaf
pepper
mixed salad leaves and cherry tomatoes, to serve

TO GARNISH

ground paprika

sprigs of fresh herbs

1 Melt the butter in a small frying pan and gently fry the garlic and spring onions together for 3–4 minutes, until softened. Allow to cool.

2 Beat the soft cheese in a bowl, then add the garlic and spring onions. Stir in the herbs and season with pepper to taste, mixing well.

3 Add the Cheddar and work the mixture together to form a stiff paste. Cover and chill until ready to serve.

4 To make the Melba toast, toast the slices of bread on both sides, and then cut off the crusts.

5 Using a sharp bread knife, cut through the slices horizontally to make very thin slices.

6 Cut into triangles and then lightly grill the untoasted sides.

7 Arrange the mixed salad leaves on 4 serving plates with the cherry tomatoes. Pile the cheese pâté on top and sprinkle with a little paprika. Garnish with sprigs of fresh herbs and serve with the Melba toast.

Tomato, Olive & Mozzarella Bruschetta

These simple toasts are filled with colour and flavour. They are great as a speedy starter or delicious as an appetiser with a good red wine.

Serves 4

4 muffins

4 garlic cloves, crushed

2 tbsp butter

1 tbsp chopped basil

4 large, ripe tomatoes

1 tbsp tomato purée

8 pitted black olives, halved

salt and pepper

50 g/1¾ oz Mozzarella cheese, sliced

fresh basil leaves, to garnish

DRESSING

1 tbsp olive oil

2 tsp lemon juice

1 tsp clear honey

1 Cut the muffins in half to give eight thick pieces. Toast the muffin halves under a hot grill for 2–3 minutes until golden.

2 Mix the garlic, butter and basil together and spread on to each muffin half.

3 Cut a cross shape at the base of each tomato. Plunge the tomatoes in a bowl of boiling water – this will make the skin easier to peel. After a few minutes, pick each tomato up with a fork and peel away the skin. Chop the tomato flesh and mix with the tomato purée and olives. Divide the mixture between the muffins.

4 Mix the dressing ingredients and drizzle over each muffin. Arrange the Mozzarella cheese on top and season.

5 Return the muffins to the grill for 1–2 minutes until the cheese melts.

6 Garnish with fresh basil leaves and serve at once.

COOK'S VARIATION

Use balsamic vinegar instead of the lemon juice for an authentic Mediterranean flavour.

Mint & Cannellini Bean Dip

This dip is ideal for pre-dinner drinks or for handing around at a party,
accompanied by crisps and colourful vegetable crudités.

Serves 6

175 g/6 oz dried
cannellini beans
1 small garlic clove, crushed
1 bunch spring onions,
chopped roughly
handful of fresh mint leaves
2 tbsp tahini
(sesame seed paste)
2 tbsp olive oil
1 tsp ground cumin
1 tsp ground coriander
lemon juice
salt and pepper
sprigs of fresh mint, to garnish

TO SERVE

fresh vegetable crudités,
such as cauliflower florets,
carrots, cucumber, radishes
and peppers

1 Soak the cannellini beans overnight
in plenty of cold water.

2 Rinse and drain the beans, put
them into a large saucepan and cover
them with cold water. Bring to the
boil and boil rapidly for 10 minutes.
Reduce the heat, cover and simmer
until tender.

3 Drain the beans and transfer them
to a bowl or food processor. Add the
garlic, spring onions, mint, tahini and
olive oil.

4 Blend the mixture for about
15 seconds, or mash well by hand,
until smooth.

5 Transfer the mixture to a bowl and
season with cumin, ground coriander,
lemon juice, salt and pepper,
according to taste. Mix well, cover and
leave in a cool place for 30 minutes to
allow the flavours to develop.

6 Spoon the dip into serving bowls,
garnish with sprigs of fresh mint and
surround with vegetable crudités.

Crispy Potato Skins

Potato skins are always a favourite. Prepare the skins in advance and warm through before serving with the salad fillings.

Serves 4

4 large baking potatoes
2 tbsp vegetable oil
4 tsp salt
150 ml/¼ pint soured cream and
2 tbsp chopped chives, to serve

BEANSPROUT SALAD

50 g/1¾ oz beansprouts
1 celery stick, sliced
1 orange, peeled
and segmented
1 red dessert apple, chopped
½ red pepper, chopped
1 tbsp chopped parsley
1 tbsp light soy sauce
1 tbsp clear honey
1 small garlic clove, crushed

BEAN FILLING

100 g/3½ oz canned,
mixed beans, drained
1 onion, halved and sliced
1 tomato, chopped
2 spring onions, chopped
2 tsp lemon juice
salt and pepper

1 Scrub the potatoes and put on a baking sheet. Prick the potatoes all over with a fork and rub the oil and salt into the skin. Cook in a preheated oven at 200°C/400°F/Gas Mark 6 for 1 hour or until soft.

2 Cut the potatoes in half lengthwise and scoop out the flesh, leaving a 1 cm/½ inch thick shell. Put the shells, skin side uppermost, in the oven for 10 minutes until crisp.

3 Mix the ingredients for the beansprout salad in a bowl, tossing in the soy, honey and garlic to coat.

4 Mix the ingredients for the bean filling in a separate bowl.

5 Mix the soured cream and chives in another bowl.

6 Serve the potato skins hot, with the two salad fillings and the sour cream and chives.

Mixed Bean Pâté

This is a really quick starter to prepare if canned beans are used.
Choose a wide variety of beans for colour and flavour or use a can of mixed beans.

Serves 4
400 g/14 oz can mixed beans, drained
2 tbsp olive oil
juice of 1 lemon
2 garlic cloves, crushed
1 tbsp chopped fresh coriander
2 spring onions, chopped
salt and pepper
shredded spring onions, to garnish

1 Rinse the beans under cold running water and drain well.

2 Transfer the beans to a food processor or blender. Alternatively, place in a bowl and mash with a fork or potato masher.

3 Add the olive oil, lemon juice, garlic, and spring onions and blend until fairly smooth. Season with salt and pepper to taste.

4 Transfer the pâté to a serving bowl and chill for at least 30 minutes. Garnish with shredded spring onions and serve.

COOK'S TIP

Serve the pâté with warm pitta bread or granary toast.

Onions à la Grecque

This is a well known method of cooking vegetables and is perfect
with shallots or onions, served with a crisp salad.

Serves 4
450 g/1 lb shallots
3 tbsp olive oil
3 tbsp clear honey
2 tbsp garlic wine vinegar
3 tbsp dry white wine
1 tbsp tomato purée
2 celery stalks, sliced
2 tomatoes, seeded and chopped
2 tbsp ground coriander
chopped celery leaves, to garnish

1 Peel the shallots. Heat the oil in a
large saucepan and cook the shallots,
stirring, for 3–5 minutes or until they
begin to brown.

2 Add the honey and cook for a
further 30 seconds over a high heat,
then add the vinegar, wine and
tomato purée, stirring well.

3 Stir in the celery and tomatoes and
bring the mixture to the boil. Cook
over a high heat for 5–6 minutes.
Season with salt and pepper to taste
and leave to cool slightly.

4 Garnish with chopped celery leaves
and serve warm or cold from the
refrigerator.

COOK'S VARIATION

Use button mushrooms instead
of the shallots and fennel instead of
the celery for another
great starter.

Peppers with Rosemary Baste

The flavour of grilled or roasted peppers is very different
from when they are eaten raw, so do try them cooked in this way.

Serves 4
4 tbsp olive oil
finely grated rind of 1 lemon
4 tbsp lemon juice
1 tbsp balsamic vinegar
1 tbsp crushed fresh rosemary, or 1 tsp dried rosemary
2 red peppers, halved, cored and deseeded
2 yellow peppers, halved, cored and deseeded
2 tbsp pine kernels
salt and pepper
sprigs of fresh rosemary, to garnish

1 Mix together the olive oil, lemon rind, lemon juice, vinegar and rosemary. Season with salt and pepper to taste.

2 Place the peppers, skin-side uppermost, on the rack of a grill pan lined with foil. Brush the rosemary baste over the peppers.

3 Cook the peppers under a preheated grill until the skin begins to char, basting frequently with the rosemary baste. Remove from the heat, cover with foil to trap the steam and leave for 5 minutes.

4 Meanwhile, scatter the pine kernels on to the grill rack and toast them lightly.

5 Peel the peppers, slice them into strips and place them in a warmed serving dish.

6 Sprinkle the pine kernels over the peppers and drizzle with any remaining rosemary baste. Garnish with sprigs of fresh rosemary and serve at once.

COOK'S TIP

Rosemary contains oil of camphor, which gives an aromatic flavour.

Lentil Pâté

Red lentils are used in this spicy recipe for speed as they do not require pre-soaking.
If you have other lentils, soak and pre-cook them and use instead of the red lentils.

Serves 4
1 tbsp vegetable oil, plus extra for greasing
1 onion, chopped
2 garlic cloves, crushed
1 tsp garam masala
$1/2$ tsp ground coriander
850 ml/$1^1/2$ pints vegetable stock
175 g/6 oz red lentils
1 small egg
2 tbsp milk
2 tbsp mango chutney
2 tbsp chopped parsley
chopped parsley, to garnish
salad leaves and warm toast, to serve

1 Heat the oil in a large saucepan and sauté the onion and garlic for 2–3 minutes, stirring. Add the garam masala and ground coriander and cook for a further 30 seconds.

2 Stir in the stock and lentils and bring the mixture to the boil. Reduce the heat and simmer for 20 minutes until the lentils are cooked and softened. Remove the pan from the heat and drain off any excess moisture.

3 Put the mixture in a food processor and add the egg, milk, mango chutney and parsley. Blend for 20 seconds until smooth.

4 Grease and line the base of a 450 g/1 lb loaf tin and spoon the mixture into the tin, levelling the surface with the back of a spoon. Cover and cook in a preheated oven at 200°C/400°F/Gas Mark 6 for 40–45 minutes or until firm to the touch.

5 Allow the pâté to cool in the tin for 20 minutes, then transfer to the refrigerator to cool completely.

6 Turn out the pâté on to a serving plate, slice and garnish with chopped parsley. Serve with salad leaves and warm toast.

COOK'S VARIATION

Use other spices, such as chilli powder or Chinese five spice powder, to flavour the pâté and add tomato relish or chilli relish instead of the mango chutney, if you prefer.

Roasted Vegetables on Muffins

Roasted vegetables are delicious and attractive. Served on warm muffins
with a herb sauce, they are unbeatable.

Serves 4
1 red onion, cut into eight
1 aubergine, halved and sliced
1 yellow pepper, sliced
1 courgette, sliced
4 tbsp olive oil
1 tbsp garlic vinegar
2 tbsp vermouth
2 garlic cloves, crushed
1 tbsp chopped thyme
2 tsp light brown sugar
4 muffins, halved
salt and pepper
fresh herbs, to garnish

SAUCE
2 tbsp butter
1 tbsp flour
150 ml/$\frac{1}{4}$ pint milk
85 ml/3 fl oz vegetable stock
75 g/2$\frac{3}{4}$ oz vegetarian Cheddar, grated
1 tsp wholegrain mustard
3 tbsp chopped mixed herbs

1 Arrange the vegetables in a shallow ovenproof dish. Mix the oil, vinegar, vermouth, garlic, thyme and sugar together and pour over the vegetables. Leave to marinate for 1 hour.

2 Transfer the vegetables to a baking sheet. Cook in a pre-heated oven at 200°C/400°F/Gas Mark 6 for 20–25 minutes or until softened.

3 Meanwhile, make the sauce. Melt the butter in a small pan and add the flour. Cook for 1 minute and remove from the heat. Stir in the milk and

stock and return the pan to the heat. Bring to the boil, stirring, until thickened. Stir in the cheese, mustard and mixed herbs and season well.

4 Preheat the grill to high. Cut the muffins in half and grill for

2–3 minutes until golden brown, then remove and arrange on a serving plate.

5 Spoon the roasted vegetables on to the muffins and pour the sauce over the top. Garnish with fresh herbs and serve immediately.

Mushroom & Garlic Soufflés

These individual soufflés are very impressive starters, but must be cooked just before serving to prevent them sinking.

Serves 4
50 g/1¾ oz butter
75 g/2¾ oz flat mushrooms, chopped
2 tsp lime juice
2 garlic cloves, crushed
2 tbsp chopped marjoram
25 g/1 oz plain flour
225 ml/8 fl oz milk
salt and pepper
2 eggs, separated

1 Lightly grease the inside of four 150 ml/¼ pint individual soufflé dishes with a little butter.

2 Melt 25 g/1 oz of the butter in a frying pan. Add the mushrooms, lime juice and garlic and sauté for 2–3 minutes. Remove the mushroom mixture from the frying pan with a slotted spoon and transfer to a mixing bowl. Stir in the marjoram.

3 Melt the remaining butter in a pan. Add the flour and cook for 1 minute, then remove from the heat. Stir in the milk and return to the heat. Bring to the boil, stirring until thickened.

4 Add the sauce to the mushroom mixture, mixing well and beat in the egg yolks.

5 Whisk the egg whites until peaking and fold into the mushroom mixture until fully incorporated.

6 Divide the mixture between the soufflé dishes. Place the dishes on a baking sheet and cook in a preheated oven, 200°C/400°F/Gas Mark 6, for 8–10 minutes or until the soufflés have risen and are cooked through. Serve immediately.

COOK'S TIP

Insert a skewer into the centre of the soufflés to test if they are cooked through – it should come out clean. If not, cook for a few minutes longer, but do not overcook otherwise they will become rubbery.

Aubergine Timbale

This is a great way to serve pasta as a starter, wrapped in an aubergine mould. It looks really impressive but it is so easy to make.

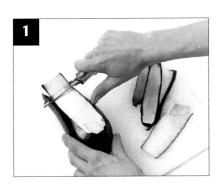

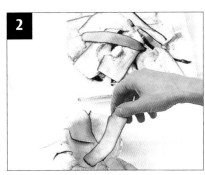

Serves 4

1 large aubergine
50 g/1¾ oz macaroni
1 tbsp vegetable oil
1 onion, chopped
2 garlic cloves, crushed
2 tbsp drained canned sweetcorn
2 tbsp frozen peas, thawed
100 g/3½ oz spinach
25 g/1 oz vegetarian Cheddar, grated
1 egg, beaten
225 g/8 oz canned, chopped tomatoes
1 tbsp chopped basil
salt and pepper

SAUCE

4 tbsp olive oil
2 tbsp white wine vinegar
2 garlic cloves, crushed
3 tbsp chopped basil
1 tbsp caster sugar

1 Cut the aubergine lengthwise into thin strips, using a potato peeler. Place in a bowl of salted boiling water and leave to stand for 3–4 minutes. Drain well.

2 Lightly grease four 150 ml/¼ pint individual ramekin dishes and use the aubergine slices to line the dishes, leaving 2.5 cm/1 inch of aubergine overlapping.

3 Cook the pasta in a pan of boiling water for 8–10 minutes or until 'al dente'. Drain. Heat the oil in a pan and sauté the onion and garlic for 2–3 minutes. Stir in the sweetcorn and peas and remove from the heat.

4 Blanch the spinach, drain well, chop and reserve. Add the pasta to the onion mixture with the cheese, egg, tomatoes and basil. Season and mix. Half-fill each ramekin with some of the pasta. Spoon the spinach on top and then the remaining pasta mixture. Fold the aubergine over the pasta

filling to cover. Put the ramekins in a roasting tin half-filled with boiling water, cover and cook in a preheated oven, 180°C/350°F/Gas Mark 4, for 20–25 minutes or until set. Meanwhile, heat the ingredients for the sauce in a pan. Turn out the ramekins and serve with the sauce.

Carrot, Fennel & Potato Medley

This is a colourful dish of shredded vegetables in a fresh garlic and honey dressing.
It is delicious served with crusty bread to mop up the dressing.

Serves 4

2 tbsp olive oil

1 potato, cut into thin strips

1 fennel bulb, cut into
thin strips

2 carrots, grated

1 red onion, cut into
thin strips

chopped chives and fennel fronds, to
garnish

DRESSING

3 tbsp olive oil

1 tbsp garlic wine vinegar

1 garlic clove, crushed

1 tsp Dijon mustard

2 tsp clear honey

salt and pepper

1 Heat the oil in a frying pan and cook the potato and fennel slices for 2–3 minutes until beginning to brown. Remove with a slotted spoon and drain on kitchen paper.

2 Arrange the carrot, red onion and potato and fennel on a serving platter.

3 Mix the dressing ingredients together and pour over the vegetables. Toss well and sprinkle with chopped chives and fennel fronds.

COOK'S VARIATION

Use mixed, grilled peppers or shredded leeks in this dish for variety, or add beansprouts and a segmented orange, if you prefer.

Light Meals

The ability to rustle up a quick light meal can be very important in our busy lives. Sometimes we may not feel like eating a full-scale meal but nevertheless want something appetizing and satisfying. Or, if lunch or dinner is going to be served late, then we may want something to tide us over.

Whatever the occasion, you're guaranteed to find a mouthwatering collection of recipes in this chapter. The recipes cater for all tastes and times of day. Many of the recipes can be prepared way

ahead of time and will not detain you in the kitchen for too long.

With such a versatile selection of recipes to choose from, using a wide range of exciting flavours and ingredients, you will easily find something to satisfy your hunger, with hardly a sandwich in sight!

Roman Focaccia

Roman focaccia makes a delicious snack on its own or
serve it with salad for a quick supper.

Makes 16 squares
7 g/^{1}/$_4$ oz dried yeast
1 tsp sugar
300 ml/^{1}/$_2$ pint hand-hot water
450 g/1 lb strong flour
2 tsp salt
3 tbsp rosemary, chopped
2 tbsp olive oil
450 g/1 lb mixed red and white onions, sliced into rings
4 garlic cloves, sliced

1 Place the yeast and sugar in a small bowl with 100 ml/3^1/$_2$ fl oz of the water. Leave to ferment in a warm place for 15 minutes.

2 Mix the flour with the salt in a large bowl.

3 Add the yeast mixture, half of the rosemary and the remaining water and mix to form a smooth dough. Knead the dough for 4 minutes.

4 Cover the dough with oiled cling film and leave to rise for about 30 minutes or until doubled in size.

5 Meanwhile, heat the oil in a large pan. Add the onions and garlic and fry for 5 minutes or until softened. Cover the pan and continue to cook for a further 7–8 minutes or until the onions are lightly caramelized.

6 Remove the cling film from the dough and knead the dough again for 1–2 minutes.

7 Roll the dough out to form a square shape. The dough should be no more than 6 mm/^{1}/$_4$ inch thick because it will rise during cooking.

8 Place the dough on to a large baking sheet, pushing out the edges until even.

9 Spread the caramelized onions over the dough, and sprinkle with the remaining rosemary. Bake the focaccia in a preheated oven, 200°C/400°F/Gas Mark 6, for 25–30 minutes or until golden. Cut the Roman focaccia into 16 squares and serve immediately.

Vegetable Samosas

These Indian snacks are perfect for a quick or light meal.
Served with a salad they can be made in advance and frozen for ease.

Makes 12
FILLING
2 tbsp vegetable oil
1 onion, chopped
$^1/_2$ tsp ground coriander
$^1/_2$ tsp ground cumin
pinch of turmeric
$^1/_2$ tsp ground ginger
$^1/_2$ tsp garam masala
1 garlic clove, crushed
225 g/8 oz potatoes, diced
100 g/3$^1/_2$ oz frozen peas, thawed
150 g/5$^1/_2$ oz spinach, chopped
PASTRY
12 sheets filo pastry
oil, for deep-frying

1 To make the filling, heat the oil in a frying pan and sauté the onion for 1–2 minutes, stirring until softened. Stir in all of the spices and garlic and cook for 1 minute.

2 Add the potatoes and cook over a gentle heat for 5 minutes, stirring until they begin to soften.

3 Stir in the peas and spinach and cook for a further 3–4 minutes.

4 Lay the filo pastry sheets out on a clean work surface and fold each sheet in half lengthwise.

5 Place 2 tbsp of the vegetable filling at one end of each folded pastry sheet. Fold over one corner to make a triangle. Continue folding in this way to make a triangular package and seal the edges with water. Repeat with the remaining pastry and filling.

6 Heat the oil for deep-frying to 180°C/350°F or until a cube of bread browns in 30 seconds. Fry the samosas, in batches, for 1–2 minutes until golden. Drain on absorbent kitchen paper and keep warm whilst cooking the remainder. Serve.

COOK'S TIP

Serve with natural yogurt
and a salad.

Tofu Stuffed Mushrooms

Use large open-capped mushrooms for this recipe
for their flavour and suitability for filling.

Serves 4
8 open-capped mushrooms
1 tbsp olive oil
1 small leek, chopped
1 celery stick, chopped
100 g/3$^{1}/_{2}$ oz firm tofu, diced
1 courgette, chopped
1 carrot, chopped
100 g/3$^{1}/_{2}$ oz wholemeal breadcrumbs
2 tbsp chopped basil
1 tbsp tomato purée
2 tbsp pine nuts
75 g/2$^{3}/_{4}$ oz vegetarian Cheddar cheese, grated
150 ml/$^{1}/_{4}$ pint vegetable stock
salt and pepper
green salad, to serve

1 Remove the stalks from the mushrooms and chop finely.

2 Heat the oil in a frying pan. Add the chopped mushroom stalks, leek, celery, tofu, courgette and carrot and cook for 3–4 minutes, stirring.

3 Stir in the breadcrumbs, basil, tomato purée and pine nuts. Season with salt and pepper to taste.

4 Spoon the mixture into the mushrooms and top with the cheese.

5 Place the mushrooms in a shallow ovenproof dish and pour the vegetable stock around them.

6 Cook in a preheated oven at 220°C/425°F/Gas Mark 7 for 20 minutes or until cooked through and the cheese has melted. Remove the mushrooms from the dish and serve immediately with a green salad.

COOK'S TIP

Vary the vegetables used for flavour and colour or according to those you have available.

Ricotta & Spinach Parcels

Ricotta and spinach make a great flavour combination,
especially when encased in light puff-pastry parcels.

Serves 4
350 g/12 oz spinach, trimmed and washed thoroughly
25 g/1 oz butter
1 small onion, chopped finely
1 tsp green peppercorns
450 g/1 lb puff pastry
250 g/9 oz Ricotta
1 egg, beaten
salt
sprigs of fresh herbs, to garnish
fresh vegetables, to serve

1 Pack the spinach into a large saucepan. Add a little salt and a very small amount of water and cook until wilted. Drain well, cool and then squeeze out any excess moisture with the back of a spoon. Chop roughly.

2 Melt the butter in a small saucepan and fry the onion gently until softened, but not browned. Add the green peppercorns and cook for 2 minutes. Remove from the heat, add the spinach and mix together.

3 Roll out the puff pastry thinly on a lightly floured work surface and cut into 4 squares, each 18 cm/7 inches across. Place a quarter of the spinach mixture in the centre of each square and top with a quarter of the cheese.

4 Brush a little beaten egg around the edges of the pastry squares and bring the corners together to form parcels. Press the edges together to seal. Lift the parcels on to a greased baking sheet, brush with beaten egg and bake in a preheated oven, 200°C/ 400°F/Gas Mark 6, for 20–25 minutes, until risen and golden.

5 Serve hot, garnished with sprigs of fresh herbs and accompanied by fresh vegetables.

Garlic Mushrooms on Toast

This is so simple to prepare and looks great if you use a variety of mushrooms for shape and texture. Cooked in garlic butter, they are simply irresistible.

Serves 4

75 g/2³/₄ oz vegetarian margarine

2 garlic cloves, crushed

350 g/12 oz mixed mushrooms, such as open-cap, button, oyster and shiitake, sliced

1 tbsp chopped parsley

8 slices French bread

salt and pepper

1 Melt the margarine in a frying pan. Add the garlic and cook for 30 seconds, stirring.

2 Add the mushrooms and cook for 5 minutes, turning occasionally.

3 Meanwhile, toast the French bread slices under a preheated medium grill for 2–3 minutes, turning once. Transfer the toasts to a serving plate.

4 Toss the parsley into the mushrooms, mixing well, and spoon the mixture over the bread. Serve immediately.

COOK'S TIP

Add seasonings, such as curry powder or chilli powder, to the mushrooms for extra flavour, if liked.

Bulgar-Filled Aubergines

In this recipe, aubergines are filled with a spicy bulgar wheat
and vegetable stuffing for a delicious light meal.

Serves 4
4 medium aubergines
salt
175 g/6 oz bulgar wheat
300 ml/^{1}/$_2$ pint boiling water
3 tbsp olive oil
2 garlic cloves, crushed
2 tbsp pine nuts
^{1}/$_2$ tsp turmeric
1 tsp chilli powder
2 celery sticks, chopped
4 spring onions, chopped
1 carrot, grated
50 g/1^3/$_4$ oz button mushrooms, chopped
2 tbsp raisins
2 tbsp chopped fresh coriander
green salad, to serve

1 Cut the aubergines in half lengthwise and scoop out the flesh with a teaspoon. Chop the flesh and set aside. Rub the insides of the aubergines with a little salt and leave to stand for 20 minutes.

2 Meanwhile, put the bulgar wheat in a mixing bowl and pour the boiling water over the top. Leave to stand for 20 minutes or until the water has been absorbed.

3 Heat the oil in a frying pan. Add the garlic, nuts, turmeric, chilli powder, celery, spring onions, carrot, mushrooms and raisins and cook for 2–3 minutes.

4 Stir in the reserved aubergine flesh and cook for a further 2–3 minutes.

Add the coriander, mixing well.

5 Remove the pan from the heat and stir in the bulgar wheat. Rinse the aubergine shells under cold water and pat dry with absorbent kitchen paper.

6 Spoon the bulgar filling into the aubergines and place in a roasting tin. Pour in a little boiling water and cook in a preheated oven, 180°C/350°F/Gas Mark 4, for 15–20 minutes.

7 Serve hot with a green salad.

Creamy Mushroom Vol-au-Vent

A simple mixture of creamy, tender mushrooms filling a crisp, rich pastry case,
this dish will make an impression at any dinner party.

Serves 4
500 g/1 lb 2 oz puff pastry, thawed if frozen
1 egg, beaten, for glazing
FILLING
25 g/1 oz butter or vegetarian margarine
750 g/1 lb 10 oz mixed mushrooms such as open-cup, field, button, chestnut, shiitake, pied de mouton, sliced
6 tbsp dry white wine
4 tbsp double cream
2 tbsp chopped fresh chervil
salt and pepper
sprigs of fresh chervil, to garnish

1 Roll out the pastry on a lightly floured surface to form a 20 cm/8 inch square.

2 Using a sharp knife, mark a square 2.5 cm/1 inch from the pastry edge, cutting halfway through the pastry.

3 Score the top of the square in a diagonal pattern. Knock up the edges with a kitchen knife and place on a baking sheet. Brush the top with beaten egg, taking care not to let the egg run into the cut edges. Bake in a preheated oven, 220°C/425°F/Gas Mark 7, for 35 minutes.

4 Cut out the central square. Scoop out the soft pastry inside the case and discard, leaving the base intact. Return to the oven, together with the central square, for about 10 minutes.

5 To make the filling, melt the butter in a frying pan and stir-fry the mushrooms for 3 minutes.

6 Add the wine and cook for 10 minutes, stirring occasionally, until the mushrooms have softened. Stir in the cream, chervil and seasoning.

7 Spoon the filling into the pastry case. Top with the pastry square, garnish and serve.

Potato, Pepper & Mushroom Hash

This is a quick one-pan dish which is ideal for a quick snack. Packed with colour
and flavour it is very versatile and you can add any other vegetable you have to hand.

Serves 4
675 g/1¹/₂ lb potatoes, cubed
1 tbsp olive oil
2 garlic cloves, crushed
1 green pepper, cubed
1 yellow pepper, cubed
3 tomatoes, diced
75 g/2³/₄ oz button mushrooms, halved
1 tbsp vegetarian Worcester sauce
2 tbsp chopped basil
salt and pepper
fresh basil sprigs, to garnish
warm, crusty bread, to serve

1 Cook the potatoes in a saucepan of boiling salted water for 7–8 minutes. Drain well and reserve.

2 Heat the oil in a large, heavy-based frying pan and cook the potatoes for 8–10 minutes, stirring until browned.

3 Add the garlic and peppers and cook for 2–3 minutes. Stir in the tomatoes and mushrooms and cook, stirring, for 5–6 minutes.

4 Stir in the vegetarian Worcester sauce and basil and season well. Garnish and serve with crusty bread.

COOK'S TIP

Most brands of Worcester sauce contain anchovies so make sure you choose a vegetarian variety.

Leek & Sun-dried Tomato Timbales

Angel-hair pasta, known as cappellini, is mixed with fried leeks, sun-dried
tomatoes, fresh oregano and beaten eggs, and baked in ramekins.

Serves 4
90 g/3 oz angel-hair pasta (cappellini)
25 g/1 oz butter
1 tbsp olive oil
1 large leek, sliced finely
60 g/2 oz sun-dried tomatoes in oil, drained and chopped
1 tbsp chopped fresh oregano or 1 tsp dried oregano
2 eggs, beaten
100 ml/3½ fl oz single cream
1 tbsp freshly grated Parmesan
salt and pepper
sprigs of oregano, to garnish
lettuce leaves, to serve

TOMATO SAUCE

1 small onion, chopped finely
1 small garlic clove, crushed
350 g/12 oz tomatoes, peeled and chopped
1 tsp mixed dried Italian herbs
4 tbsp dry white wine

1 Cook the pasta in a pan of boiling
salted water for about 3 minutes until
'al dente'. Drain and rinse with cold
water to cool quickly.

2 Meanwhile, heat the butter and oil
in a frying pan. Gently fry
the leek until softened, about 5–6
minutes. Add the sun-dried tomatoes
and oregano, and cook for a further
2 minutes. Remove from the heat.

3 Add the leek mixture to the pasta.
Stir in the beaten eggs, cream and
Parmesan and season.

4 Divide the mixture between 4
greased ramekins. Place in a roasting
tin with enough warm water to come
halfway up their sides. Bake in a
preheated oven, 180°C/350°F/Gas
Mark 4, for 30 minutes, or until set.

5 To make the sauce, fry the onion
and garlic until softened. Add the

tomatoes, herbs and wine. Cover and
cook for 20 minutes until pulpy. Blend
in a food processor or press through a
sieve until smooth.

6 Run a knife around the edge of the
ramekin dishes, then turn out the
timbales on to 4 serving plates. Pour
over a little sauce, garnish and serve.

Marinated Grilled Fennel

Fennel has a wonderful aniseed flavour which is ideal for grilling or barbecuing.
Marinated in lime, garlic, oil and mustard, this recipe is really delicious.

Serves 4
2 fennel bulbs
1 red pepper, cut into large cubes
1 lime, cut into eight wedges
MARINADE
2 tbsp lime juice
4 tbsp olive oil
2 garlic cloves, crushed
1 tsp wholegrain mustard
1 tbsp chopped thyme
fennel fronds, to garnish
crisp salad, to serve

1 Cut each of the fennel bulbs into eight pieces and place in a shallow dish. Mix in the peppers.

2 To make the marinade, combine the lime juice, oil, garlic, mustard and thyme. Pour the marinade over the fennel and peppers and leave to marinate for 1 hour.

3 Thread the fennel and peppers on to wooden skewers with the lime wedges. Preheat a grill to medium and grill the kebabs for 10 minutes, turning and basting with the marinade. Transfer to serving plates, garnish with fennel fronds and serve with a crisp salad.

COOK'S TIP

Soak the skewers in water for 20 minutes before using to prevent them from burning during cooking.

Refried Beans with Tortillas

Refried beans are a classic Mexican dish and are usually served as an accompaniment. They are, however, delicious when served with warm tortillas and a quick onion relish.

Serves 4
BEANS
2 tbsp olive oil
1 onion, finely chopped
3 garlic cloves, crushed
1 green chilli, chopped
400 g/14 oz can red kidney beans, drained
400 g/14 oz can pinto beans, drained
2 tbsp chopped coriander
150 ml/¼ pint vegetable stock
8 wheat tortillas
25 g/1 oz vegetarian Cheddar cheese, grated
salt and pepper
RELISH
4 spring onions, chopped
1 red onion, chopped
1 green chilli, chopped
1 tbsp garlic wine vinegar
1 tsp caster sugar
1 tomato, chopped

1 Heat the oil for the beans in a large frying pan. Add the onion and sauté for 3–5 minutes until softened. Add the garlic and chilli and cook for 1 minute.

2 Mash the beans with a potato masher and stir into the pan with the coriander.

3 Stir in the stock and cook the beans, stirring, for 5 minutes until soft and pulpy.

4 Place the tortillas on a baking sheet and heat through in a warm oven for 1–2 minutes. Mix the relish ingredients together.

5 Spoon the beans into a serving dish and top with the cheese. Season well. Roll the tortillas and serve with the relish and beans.

COOK'S TIP

Add a little more liquid to the beans when they are cooking if they begin to catch on the bottom of the frying pan.

Cauliflower Roulade

A light-as-air mixture of eggs and vegetables produces a stylish vegetarian
dish that can be enjoyed hot or cold.

Serves 6

1 small cauliflower, divided into florets
4 eggs, separated
90 g/3 oz Cheddar, grated
60 g/2 oz cottage cheese
large pinch of grated nutmeg
$^1/_2$ tsp mustard powder
salt and pepper

FILLING

1 bunch watercress, trimmed
60 g/2 oz butter
25 g/1 oz flour
175 ml/6 fl oz natural yogurt
25 g/1 oz Cheddar, grated
60 g/2 oz cottage cheese

1 Line a Swiss roll tin with baking
parchment. Steam the cauliflower
until just tender, then drain. Put the
cauliflower in a food processor and
finely process, or chop finely and
push through a sieve.

2 Beat the egg yolks, then stir in the
cauliflower, 60 g/2 oz of the Cheddar
and the cottage cheese. Season with
nutmeg, mustard, and salt and pepper.
Whisk the egg whites until stiff but
not dry, then fold into the cauliflower,
using a metal spoon. Spread the
mixture in the prepared tin) and bake
in a preheated oven, 200°C/400°F/Gas
Mark 6, for 20–25 minutes, until risen
and golden.

3 For the filling, chop the watercress,
reserving a few sprigs for garnish.
Melt the butter in a small pan, add
the watercress and cook for 3 minutes,

stirring, until wilted. Blend in the flour,
then stir in the yogurt and simmer for
2 minutes. Stir in the cheeses.

4 Turn out the roulade on to a damp
tea towel covered with baking
parchment. Peel off the paper and leave
for 1 minute to allow the steam to

escape. Roll up the roulade, including a
new sheet of paper, starting from one
narrow end. Unroll the roulade, spread
the filling to within 2.5 cm/1 inch of
the edges, and roll up. Transfer to a
baking sheet, sprinkle on the Cheddar
and return to the oven for 5 minutes.
Serve immediately.

Falafel

These are a very tasty, well known Middle Eastern dish of small chick-pea based balls, spiced and deep-fried. They are delicious hot with a crisp tomato salad.

Serves 4
650 g/1 lb 7 oz canned chick-peas, drained
1 red onion, chopped
3 garlic cloves, crushed
100 g/3$^{1}/_{2}$ oz wholemeal bread
2 small red chillies
1 tsp ground cumin
1 tsp ground coriander
$^{1}/_{2}$ tsp turmeric
1 tbsp chopped coriander, plus extra to garnish
1 egg, beaten
100 g/3$^{1}/_{2}$ oz wholemeal breadcrumbs
vegetable oil, for deep-frying
salt and pepper

1 Put the chick-peas, onion, garlic, bread, chillies, spices and coriander in a food processor and blend for 30 seconds. Stir and season well. Remove the mixture from the food processor and shape into walnut-sized balls.

2 Place the beaten egg in a shallow bowl. Dip the balls into the egg to coat and then roll them in the breadcrumbs, shaking off any excess.

3 Heat the oil for deep-frying to 180°C/350°F or until a cube of bread browns in 30 seconds. Fry the falafel, in batches, for 2–3 minutes until crisp and browned. Remove from the oil with a slotted spoon and dry on absorbent kitchen paper. Garnish with coriander and serve.

COOK'S TIP

Serve the falafel with a coriander and yogurt sauce. Mix 150 ml/
$^{1}/_{4}$ pint natural yogurt with 2 tbsp chopped coriander and 1 crushed garlic clove.

Ciabatta Vegetable Rolls

Sandwiches are always a welcome snack but can be quite mundane.
These crisp ciabatta rolls filled with roast peppers and cheese are irresistible
and will always be a popular light meal.

Serves 4
4 ciabatta rolls
2 tbsp olive oil
1 garlic clove crushed
FILLING
1 red pepper
1 green pepper
1 yellow pepper
4 radishes, sliced
100 g/3^1/$_2$ oz cream cheese
watercress, to serve

1 Halve the ciabatta rolls. Heat the oil and garlic in a pan. Pour the garlic and oil mixture over the cut surfaces of the rolls and leave to stand.

2 Halve the peppers and place, skin side uppermost, on a grill rack. Cook under a hot grill for 8–10 minutes until just beginning to char. Remove the peppers from the grill, peel and slice thinly.

3 Arrange the radish slices on one half of each roll with a few watercress leaves. Spoon the cream cheese on top. Pile the peppers on top of the cream cheese and top with the other half of the roll. Serve.

COOK'S TIP

Allow the peppers to cool slightly before filling the roll otherwise the cheese will melt.

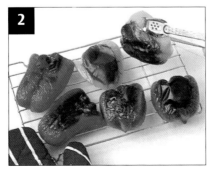

Tofu & Vegetable Mini Kebabs

Cubes of smoked tofu are speared on bamboo satay sticks with
crisp vegetables, basted with lemon juice and olive oil, and then grilled.

Serves 6

300 g/10½ oz smoked tofu,
cut into cubes

1 large red and 1 large yellow
pepper, deseeded
and cut into small squares

175 g/6 oz button mushrooms, wiped

1 small courgette, sliced

finely grated rind and juice of 1 lemon

3 tbsp olive oil

1 tbsp chopped fresh parsley

1 tsp caster sugar

salt and pepper

sprigs of parsley, to garnish

SAUCE

125 g/4½ oz cashew nuts

15 g/½ oz butter

1 garlic clove, crushed

1 shallot, chopped finely

1 tsp ground coriander

1 tsp ground cumin

1 tbsp caster sugar

1 tbsp desiccated coconut

150 ml/¼ pint natural yogurt

1 Thread the tofu cubes, peppers, mushrooms and courgettes on to bamboo satay sticks. Arrange in a shallow dish.

2 Mix together the lemon rind and juice, oil, parsley and sugar. Season with salt and pepper. Pour over the kebabs, brushing them with the mixture. Leave for 10 minutes.

3 To make the sauce, scatter the cashew nuts on to a baking sheet and toast until browned.

4 Melt the butter in a saucepan and cook the garlic and shallot gently until softened. Transfer to a blender or food processor, add the cashew nuts, ground coriander, cumin, sugar, coconut and yogurt and blend until combined, about 15 seconds. Alternatively, chop the cashew nuts very finely by hand and mix with the remaining ingredients.

5 Place the kebabs under a preheated grill and cook, turning and basting frequently with the lemon juice mixture, until lightly browned.

6 Transfer the kebabs to serving plates and garnish with sprigs of parsley. Serve with the cashew nut sauce.

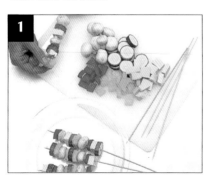

Calzone with Sun-dried Tomatoes & Vegetables

These pizza base parcels are great for making in advance and freezing – they can be defrosted when required for a quick snack.

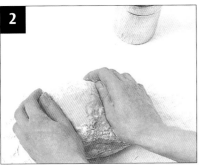

Makes 4
DOUGH
450 g/1 lb strong white flour
2 tsp easy-blend dried yeast
1 tsp caster sugar
150 ml/$^1/_4$ pint vegetable stock
150 ml/$^1/_4$ pint passata
beaten egg
FILLING
1 tbsp vegetable oil
1 onion, chopped
1 garlic clove, crushed
2 tbsp chopped sun-dried tomatoes
100 g/3$^1/_2$ oz spinach, chopped
3 tbsp canned and drained sweetcorn
25 g/1 oz French beans, cut into three
1 tbsp tomato purée
1 tbsp chopped oregano
50 g/1$^3/_4$ oz Mozzarella cheese, sliced
salt and pepper

1 Sieve the flour into a bowl. Add the yeast and sugar and beat in the stock and passata to make a smooth dough.

2 Knead the dough on a lightly floured surface for 10 minutes. Place the dough in a clean, lightly oiled bowl and leave to rise in a warm place for 1 hour or until doubled in size.

3 Meanwhile, heat the oil for the filling in a frying pan and sauté the onion for 2–3 minutes. Stir in the garlic, tomatoes, spinach, corn and beans and cook for a further 3–4 minutes, stirring. Add the tomato purée and oregano and season well.

4 Divide the risen dough into 4 equal portions and roll each on to a floured surface to form an 18 cm/7 inch circle. Spoon a quarter of the filling on to one half of each circle and top with cheese. Fold the dough over to encase the filling, sealing the edge with a fork. Glaze with beaten egg. Put the calzone on a lightly greased baking sheet and cook in a preheated oven, 220°C/425°F/Gas Mark 7, for 25–30 minutes until risen and golden. Serve warm.

Spinach Frittata

A frittata is another word for a large, thick omelette.
This is an Italian dish which may be made with many flavourings.
Spinach is used as the main ingredient in this recipe for colour and flavour.

Serves 4
450 g/1 lb spinach
2 tsp water
4 eggs, beaten
2 tbsp single cream
2 garlic cloves, crushed
50 g/1¾ oz canned sweetcorn, drained
1 celery stick, chopped
1 red chilli, chopped
2 tomatoes, seeded and diced
2 tbsp olive oil
2 tbsp butter
25 g/1 oz pecan nut halves
2 tbsp grated Pecorino cheese
25 g/1 oz Fontina cheese, cubed
a pinch of paprika

1 Cook the spinach in 2 teaspoons of water in a covered pan for 5 minutes. Drain thoroughly and pat dry on absorbent kitchen paper.

2 Beat the eggs in a bowl and stir in the spinach, cream, garlic, sweetcorn, celery, chilli and tomato.

3 Heat the oil and butter in a 20 cm/ 8 inch heavy-based frying pan.

COOK'S TIP

Be careful not to burn the underside of the frittata during the initial cooking stage – this is why it is important to use a heavy-based frying pan. Add a little extra oil to the pan when you turn the frittata over if required.

4 Spoon the egg mixture into the frying pan and sprinkle with the pecan nut halves, Pecorino and Fontina cheeses and paprika. Cook without stirring over a medium heat for 5–7 minutes or until the underside of the frittata is brown.

5 Put a large plate over the pan and invert to turn out the frittata. Slide it back into the frying pan and cook the other side for a further 2–3 minutes. Serve the frittata straight from the frying pan or transfer to a serving plate.

Aubergine
& Mushroom Satay

Grilled, skewered vegetables are served with a satay sauce.

Serves 4

2 aubergines,
cut into 2.5 cm/1 inch pieces
175 g/6 oz small chestnut mushrooms

MARINADE

1 tsp cumin seeds
1 tsp coriander seeds
2.5 cm/1 inch piece ginger root, grated
2 garlic cloves, crushed lightly
$^1/_2$ stalk lemon grass, chopped roughly
4 tbsp light soy sauce
8 tbsp sunflower oil
2 tbsp lemon juice

PEANUT SAUCE

$^1/_2$ tsp cumin seeds
$^1/_2$ tsp coriander seeds
3 garlic cloves
1 small onion, quartered
1 tbsp lemon juice
1 tsp salt
$^1/_2$ red chilli, deseeded and sliced
125 ml/4 fl oz coconut milk
250 g/9 oz crunchy peanut butter
250 ml/9 fl oz water

1 Thread the aubergines and mushrooms on to eight skewers.

2 To make the marinade, grind the cumin, coriander, ginger, garlic and lemon grass together. Add to a wok or a frying pan and stir-fry over a high heat until fragrant. Remove from the heat and add the remaining marinade ingredients.

3 Place the skewers in a non-porous dish and spoon the marinade over.

Leave to marinate for a minimum of 2 hours and up to 8 hours.

4 To make the sauce, grind together the cumin, coriander and garlic. Purée the onion in a food processor, or chop finely by hand, then add to the cumin mixture. Add the remaining ingredients, except for the water.

Transfer to a pan and blend in the water. Bring to the boil and cook until thickened. Transfer to a serving bowl.

5 Place the skewers on a baking sheet and cook under a hot grill for 15–20 minutes. Brush with the marinade and turn once. Serve with the peanut sauce.

Spinach Pancakes

Serve these pancakes as a light lunch or supper dish, with a tomato
and basil salad for a dramatic colour contrast.

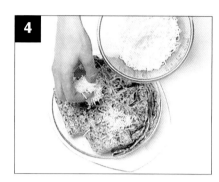

Makes 8–12 pancakes
90 g/3 oz wholemeal flour
1 egg
150 ml/¼ pint natural yogurt
3 tbsp water
1 tbsp vegetable oil
200 g/7 oz frozen leaf spinach, defrosted and liquidized
pinch of grated nutmeg
salt and pepper
lemon wedges and fresh coriander sprigs, to garnish

FILLING
1 tbsp vegetable oil
3 spring onions, thinly sliced
250 g/9 oz Ricotta
4 tbsp natural yogurt
90 g/3 oz Gruyère, grated
1 egg, lightly beaten
125 g/4½ oz unsalted cashew nuts
2 tbsp chopped fresh parsley
pinch of cayenne pepper

3 Heat the oil in a frying pan. Pour in 3–4 tbsp of the batter and tilt the pan so that it covers the base. Cook for 3 minutes, until bubbles appear in the centre. Turn and cook the other side for 2 minutes, until lightly browned. Slide the pancake on to a warm plate, cover with foil and keep warm while you cook the rest.

4 Spread a little filling over each pancake and fold in half and then half again, envelope style. Spoon the remaining filling into the opening. Grease an ovenproof dish and arrange the pancakes in a single layer. Sprinkle with the remaining cheese and cook in a preheated oven, 180°C/350°F/Gas Mark 4, for 15 minutes. Garnish and serve.

1 Sift the flour and salt into a bowl. Beat together the egg, yogurt, water and oil and gradually pour on to the flour, beating all the time. Stir in the spinach purée and season with pepper and nutmeg.

2 To make the filling, heat the oil in a pan and fry the spring onions until translucent. Remove with a slotted spoon and drain on paper towels. Beat together the Ricotta, yogurt and half the Gruyère. Beat in the egg and stir in the cashews and parsley. Season with salt and cayenne.

Mixed Vegetable Dim Sum

Dim sum are small Chinese parcels, usually served as part
of a large mixed meal. They may be filled with any variety of fillings,
steamed or fried and served with a dipping sauce.

Serves 4
2 spring onions, chopped
25 g/1 oz green beans, chopped
½ small carrot, finely chopped
1 red chilli, chopped
25 g/1 oz beansprouts, chopped
25 g/1 oz button mushrooms, chopped
25 g/1 oz unsalted cashew nuts, chopped
1 small egg, beaten
2 tbsp cornflour
1 tsp light soy sauce
1 tsp hoi-sin sauce
1 tsp sesame oil
32 wonton wrappers
oil, for deep-frying
1 tbsp sesame seeds

the wontons, in batches, for 1–2
minutes or until golden brown.
Drain on absorbent kitchen paper.

5 Sprinkle the sesame seeds over the
wontons. Serve with a soy or plum
dipping sauce.

COOK'S TIP

If preferred, arrange the wontons on a
heatproof plate and then steam in a
steamer for 5-7 minutes. for a healthier
cooking method.

1 Mix all of the vegetables together in
a bowl and stir in the nuts, egg,
cornflour, soy sauce, hoi-sin sauce
and sesame oil, mixing well.

2 Lay the wonton wrappers out on a
chopping board and spoon small
quantities of the mixture into the
centre of each.

3 Gather the wrapper around
the filling at the top, leaving the
top open.

4 Heat the oil for deep-frying in a
wok to 180°C/350°F or until a cube
of bread browns in 30 seconds. Fry

Butter-crust Tartlets with Feta Cheese

These crisp-baked bread cases, filled with sliced tomatoes,
Feta cheese, black olives and quail's eggs, are quick to make and taste delicious.

Serves 4

8 slices bread from a medium-
cut large loaf

125 g/4^1/$_2$ oz butter, melted

125 g/4^1/$_2$ oz Feta cheese,
cut into small cubes

4 cherry tomatoes,
cut into wedges

8 pitted black or green
olives, halved

8 quail's eggs, hard-boiled

2 tbsp olive oil

1 tbsp wine vinegar

1 tsp wholegrain mustard

pinch of caster sugar

salt and pepper

fresh parsley sprigs, to garnish

1 Remove the crusts from the bread. Trim the bread into squares and flatten each piece with a rolling pin.

2 Brush the bread with melted butter, and then arrange them in bun or muffin tins. Press a piece of crumpled foil into each bread case to secure in place. Bake in a preheated oven, 190°C/375°F/Gas Mark 5, for about 10 minutes, or until crisp and browned.

3 Meanwhile, mix together the Feta cheese, tomatoes and olives. Shell the eggs and quarter them. Mix together the olive oil, vinegar, mustard and sugar. Season with salt and pepper.

4 Remove the bread cases from the oven and discard the foil. Leave to cool slightly.

5 Just before serving, fill the bread cases with the cheese and tomato mixture. Arrange the eggs on top and spoon over the mustard dressing. Garnish with parsley sprigs and serve immediately.

COOK'S TIP

Feta cheese is made from sheep or goat's milk. It is curdled naturally without the addition of rennet.

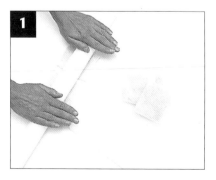

Crisp-Fried Vegetables with Hot & Sweet Dipping Sauce

A Thai-style dipping sauce makes the perfect accompaniment
to fresh vegetables coated in a light batter and deep-fried.

Serves 4

vegetable oil, for deep-frying
500 g/1 lb 2 oz selection of vegetables,
such as cauliflower, broccoli,
mushrooms, courgettes, peppers and baby
sweetcorn cobs, cut into even-sized pieces

BATTER

125 g/4$^{1}/_{2}$ oz plain flour
$^{1}/_{2}$ tsp salt
1 tsp caster sugar
1 tsp baking powder
3 tbsp vegetable oil
200 ml/7 fl oz warm water

SAUCE

6 tbsp light malt vinegar
2 tbsp Thai fish sauce or light soy sauce
2 tbsp water
1 tbsp soft brown sugar
pinch of salt
2 garlic cloves, crushed
2 tsp grated ginger root
2 red chillies, deseeded and chopped finely
2 tbsp chopped fresh coriander

1 To make the batter, sift the flour, salt, sugar and baking powder into a large bowl. Add the oil and most of the water. Whisk together to make a smooth batter, adding extra water to give it the consistency of single cream. Chill for 20–30 minutes.

2 Meanwhile, make the sauce. Heat the vinegar, fish sauce or soy sauce, water, sugar and salt until boiling. Remove from the heat and leave to cool.

3 Mix together the garlic, ginger, chillies and coriander in a small serving bowl. Add the cooled vinegar mixture and stir together.

4 Heat the vegetable oil for deep-frying in a wok or deep-fryer. Dip the prepared vegetables in the batter and fry them, a few at a time, until crisp and golden – about 2 minutes. Drain on paper towels.

5 Serve the vegetables accompanied by the dipping sauce.

Watercress & Cheese Tartlets

These individual tartlets are great for lunchtime or for picnic food. Watercress is a good source of folic acid, which is important in early pregnancy.

Makes 4
100 g/3^1/$_2$ oz plain flour
pinch of salt
75 g/2^3/$_4$ oz butter or vegetarian margarine
2–3 tbsp cold water
2 bunches watercress
2 garlic cloves, crushed
1 shallot, chopped
150 g/5^1/$_2$ oz Cheddar cheese, grated
4 tbsp natural yogurt
^{1}/$_2$ tsp paprika

1 Sieve the flour into a bowl and add the salt. Rub 50 g/1^3/$_4$ oz of the butter or margarine into the flour until the mixture resembles breadcrumbs. Stir in the cold water to make a dough.

2 Roll the dough out on a floured surface and use to line four 10 cm/ 4 inch tartlet tins. Prick the bases with a fork and leave to chill.

3 Heat the remaining butter or margarine in a frying pan. Discard the stems from the watercress and add to the pan with the garlic and shallot, cooking for 1–2 minutes until the watercress is wilted. Remove the pan from the heat and stir in the cheese, yogurt and paprika. Spoon the mixture into the pastry cases and cook in a preheated oven, 180°C/350°F/Gas Mark 4, for 20 minutes or until the filling is firm. Turn out the tartlets and serve.

VARIATION

Use spinach instead of the watercress, making sure it is well drained before mixing with the remaining filling ingredients.

Vegetable Enchiladas

This Mexican dish uses prepared tortillas which are readily available in supermarkets.
They are filled with a spicy vegetable mixture and topped with a hot tomato sauce.

Serves 4
4 flour tortillas
75 g/2³/₄ oz Cheddar, grated

FILLING
75 g/2³/₄ oz spinach
2 tbsp olive oil
8 baby sweetcorn cobs, sliced
25 g/1 oz frozen peas, thawed
1 red pepper, diced
1 carrot, diced
1 leek, sliced
2 garlic cloves, crushed
1 red chilli, chopped
salt and pepper

SAUCE
300 ml/¹/₂ pint passata
2 shallots, chopped
1 garlic clove, crushed
300 ml/¹/₂ pint vegetable stock
1 tsp caster sugar
1 tsp chilli powder

1 To make the filling, blanch the spinach in a pan of boiling water for 2 minutes, drain well and chop.

2 Heat the oil in a frying pan and sauté the corn, peas, pepper, carrot, leek, garlic and chilli for 3–4 minutes. Stir in the spinach and season well.

3 Put all of the sauce ingredients in a saucepan and bring to the boil, stirring. Cook over a high heat for 20 minutes, stirring, until thickened and reduced by a third.

4 Spoon a quarter of the filling along the centre of each tortilla.

5 Roll the tortillas around the filling and place in an ovenproof dish, seam-side down.

6 Pour the sauce over the tortillas and sprinkle the cheese on top. Cook in a preheated oven, 180°C/350°F/Gas Mark 4, for 20 minutes or until the cheese has melted and browned. Serve immediately.

Mediterranean Vegetable Tart

A rich tomato pastry base topped with a mouthwatering selection of vegetables
and cheese makes a dish that's tasty as well as attractive.

Serves 6
1 aubergine, sliced
2 tbsp salt
4 tbsp olive oil
1 garlic clove, crushed
1 large yellow pepper, deseeded and sliced
300 ml/^{1}/$_{2}$ pint ready-made tomato pasta sauce
125 g/4^{1}/$_{2}$ oz sun-dried tomatoes in oil, drained and halved if necessary
175 g/6 oz Mozzarella, drained and sliced thinly
PASTRY
225 g/8 oz plain flour
pinch of celery salt
125 g/4^{1}/$_{2}$ oz butter or vegetarian margarine
2 tbsp tomato purée
2–3 tbsp milk

1 To make the pastry, sift the flour and celery salt into a bowl. Rub in the butter or margarine until the mixture resembles fine breadcrumbs. Mix the tomato purée and milk and stir into the mixture to form a firm dough. Knead on a floured surface until smooth. Wrap and chill for 30 minutes.

2 Grease a 28 cm/11 inch loose-bottomed flan tin. Roll out the pastry on a floured surface and use to line the tin. Trim and prick all over with a fork. Chill for 30 minutes.

3 Layer the aubergine in a dish, sprinkling with the salt. Leave for 30 minutes.

4 Bake the pastry case in a preheated oven, 200°C/400°F/Gas Mark 6, for 20–25 minutes until cooked and golden. Remove from the oven and set aside. Increase the oven temperature to 230°C/450°F/Gas Mark 8.

5 Rinse the aubergine and pat dry. Heat 3 tbsp of the oil in a frying pan and fry the garlic, aubergine and pepper for 5–6 minutes until softened. Drain well. Spread the pasta sauce over the pastry case and arrange the cooked vegetables, sun-dried tomatoes and Mozzarella on top. Brush with oil and bake for 5 minutes until the cheese is just melting. Serve.

Cheese & Garlic Mushroom Pizza

This pizza dough is flavoured with garlic and herbs and topped with
mixed mushrooms and melting cheese for a really delicious pizza.

Serves 4
DOUGH
450 g/1 lb strong white flour
2 tsp easy-blend yeast
2 garlic cloves, crushed
2 tbsp chopped thyme
2 tbsp olive oil
300 ml/½ pint tepid water
TOPPING
25 g/1 oz butter or vegetarian margarine
350 g/12 oz mixed mushrooms, sliced
2 garlic cloves, crushed
2 tbsp chopped parsley
2 tbsp tomato purée
6 tbsp passata
75 g/2¾ oz Mozzarella cheese, grated
salt and pepper
chopped parsley, to garnish

1 Put the flour, yeast, garlic and thyme in a mixing bowl. Make a well in the centre and gradually stir in the oil and water. Bring together to form a soft dough.

2 Turn the dough on to a floured surface and knead for 5 minutes or until smooth. Roll into a 35 cm/14 inch round and place on a greased baking sheet. Leave in a warm place for 20 minutes or until the dough puffs up.

3 Meanwhile, make the topping. Melt the margarine or butter in a frying pan and sauté the mushrooms, garlic and parsley for 5 minutes. Mix the tomato purée and passata and spoon on to the pizza base, leaving a 1 cm/½ inch edge of dough. Spoon the mushroom mixture on top. Season well and sprinkle the cheese on top. Cook the pizza in a preheated oven, 190°C/375°F/Gas Mark 5, for 20–25 minutes or until the base is crisp and the cheese has melted. Garnish with chopped parsley and serve.

COOK'S TIP

If preferred, spread the base with a prepared cheese sauce before adding the mushrooms.

Fried Tofu with Peanut Sauce

This is a very sociable dish if put in the centre of the table
where people can help themselves with cocktail sticks.

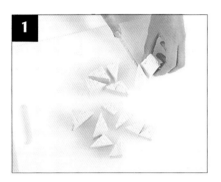

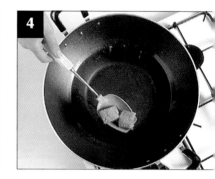

Serves 4
500 g/1 lb 2 oz marinated or plain tofu
1 litre/1³/₄ pints sunflower oil
2 tbsp sesame oil

BATTER

4 tbsp plain flour
2 eggs, beaten
4 tbsp milk
¹/₂ tsp baking powder
¹/₂ tsp chilli powder

PEANUT SAUCE

2 tbsp rice vinegar
2 tbsp sugar
1 tsp salt
3 tbsp smooth peanut butter
¹/₂ tsp chilli flakes
3 tbsp barbecue sauce

wok until a light haze appears on top.
Dip the tofu triangles into the batter
and deep-fry until golden. Drain and
serve with the sauce.

COOK'S TIP

Tofu is rich in protein, iron, calcium
and B vitamins.

1 Cut the tofu into 2.5 cm/1 inch
triangles. Set aside until required.

2 To make the sauce, combine the
vinegar, sugar and salt in a saucepan.
Bring to the boil and then simmer for
2 minutes. Remove from the heat and
add the peanut butter, chilli flakes
and barbecue sauce, stirring to mix.

3 To make the batter, sift the flour
into a bowl. Make a well in the centre
and add the eggs. Draw in the flour,
adding the milk slowly. Add the
baking powder and chilli powder,
stirring to form a batter.

4 Heat the oils in a deep-fryer or large

Baked Aubergine, Basil & Mozzarella Rolls

Thin slices of aubergine are fried in olive oil and garlic,
and then topped with pesto sauce and finely sliced Mozzarella.

Serves 4
2 aubergines, sliced thinly lengthwise
5 tbsp olive oil
1 garlic clove, crushed
4 tbsp pesto
175 g/6 oz Mozzarella, grated
basil leaves, torn into pieces
salt and pepper
fresh basil leaves, to garnish

1 Sprinkle the aubergine slices liberally with salt and leave for 10–15 minutes to extract the bitter juices. Turn the slices over and repeat. Rinse well with cold water and drain thoroughly on paper towels.

2 Heat the olive oil in a large frying pan and add the garlic. Add the aubergine slices, in batches, and fry lightly on both sides. Drain well on paper towels.

3 Spread the pesto on to one side of the aubergine slices.

4 Top with the grated Mozzarella and sprinkle with the torn basil leaves. Season with a little salt and pepper to taste.

5 Roll up the slices and secure with wooden cocktail sticks.

6 Arrange the aubergine rolls in a greased ovenproof baking dish and cook in a preheated oven, 180°C/350°F/Gas Mark 4, for about 8–10 minutes.

7 Transfer the baked aubergine, basil and Mozzarella rolls to a warmed serving plate.

8 Scatter with fresh basil leaves and serve at once.

COOK'S TIP

You may find it easier to slice the Mozzarella rather than grate it yourself.

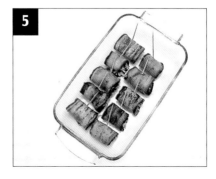

Barbecue Bean Burgers

These tasty burgers are ideal for a barbecue in the summer but they
are equally delicious cooked indoors at any time of year.

Serves 6

125 g/4½ oz aduki beans

125 g/4½ oz black-eye beans

6 tbsp vegetable oil

1 large onion, chopped finely

1 tsp yeast extract

125 g/4½ oz grated carrot

90 g/3 oz fresh wholemeal breadcrumbs

2 tbsp wholemeal flour

salt and pepper

BARBECUE SAUCE

⅓ tsp chilli powder

1 tsp celery salt

2 tbsp light muscovado sugar

2 tbsp red wine vinegar

2 tbsp vegetarian Worcestershire sauce

3 tbsp tomato purée

dash of Tabasco sauce

TO SERVE

6 wholemeal baps, toasted

mixed green salad

jacket potato fries

1 Place the beans in separate saucepans, cover with water and bring to the boil. Cover and simmer the aduki beans for 40 minutes and the black-eye beans for 50 minutes, or until tender. Drain and rinse well.

2 Transfer to a mixing bowl and lightly mash together with a potato masher or fork. Set aside.

3 Heat 1 tablespoon of the oil in a frying pan and gently fry the onion for 3–4 minutes until softened. Mix into the beans with the yeast extract,

grated carrot, breadcrumbs and seasoning. Bind together well.

4 With wet hands, divide the mixture into 6 and form into burgers 8 cm/3½ inches in diameter. Put the flour on a plate and use to coat the burgers.

5 Heat the remaining oil in a large frying pan and cook the burgers for 3–4 minutes on each side, turning

carefully, until golden and crisp. Drain on paper towels.

6 Meanwhile, make the sauce. Mix all the ingredients together until well blended. Place the burgers in the toasted baps and serve with a mixed green salad, jacket potato fries and a spoonful of the barbecue sauce.

Naan Bread with Curried Vegetable Kebabs

Warmed Indian bread is served with barbecued vegetable kebabs, which are brushed with a curry-spiced yogurt baste.

Serves 4
naan bread, to serve
sprigs of fresh mint, to garnish

YOGURT BASTE

150 ml/¼ pint natural yogurt
1 tbsp chopped fresh mint
or 1 tsp dried mint
1 tsp ground cumin
1 tsp ground coriander
½ tsp chilli powder
pinch of turmeric
pinch of ground ginger
salt and pepper

KEBABS

8 small new potatoes
1 small aubergine
1 courgette, cut into chunks
8 chestnut or closed-
cup mushrooms
8 small tomatoes

1 To make the spiced yogurt baste, mix together the yogurt, mint, cumin, coriander, chilli powder, turmeric and ginger. Season with salt and pepper, cover and chill.

2 Cook the potatoes in a saucepan of boiling water until just tender. Chop the aubergine into chunks and sprinkle them liberally with salt. Leave for 10–15 minutes to extract the bitter juices. Rinse and drain them well. Drain the potatoes.

3 If using wooden skewers, soak them in warm water for 30 minutes. Thread all of the vegetables on to 4 metal or wooden skewers, alternating the different types of vegetables.

4 Place the kebabs in a shallow dish and brush with the yogurt baste, coating them evenly. Cover and chill until ready to cook.

5 Wrap the naan bread in foil and place towards one side of the barbecue to warm through.

6 Cook the kebabs over the barbecue, basting with any remaining spiced yogurt, until they just begin to char slightly. Serve with the warmed naan bread, garnished with sprigs of fresh mint.

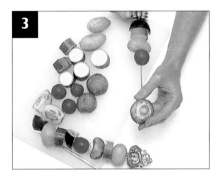

Pasta Dishes

Pasta is one of the most popular and versatile foods on sale today. Available fresh or dried, pasta is made in a wide variety of colours and flavours, shapes and sizes, each lending itself to a particular type of sauce. For instance, flat ribbons go well with cream or cheese-based sauces; tubes and shapes are ideal for trapping chunkier sauces in their crevices.

Wholewheat pastas have a chewier texture and are valuable for the additional fibre they contain. Pasta is a marvellous convenience food – both nourishing and satisfying. All types of pasta are quick to cook and provide good basic food that can be dressed up in all kinds of ways. Pasta combines very well with vegetables, herbs, nuts and cheeses, to provide scores of interesting and tasty vegetarian meals.

Vegetable Pasta Nests

These large pasta nests look impressive when presented filled
with grilled mixed vegetables, and taste delicious with the herb sauce.

Serves 4

175 g/6 oz spaghetti
1 aubergine, halved and sliced
1 courgette, diced
1 red pepper, seeded and
chopped diagonally
6 tbsp olive oil
2 garlic cloves, crushed
50 g/1¾ oz butter or
vegetarian margarine, melted
15 g/½ oz dry white breadcrumbs
salt and pepper
fresh parsley sprigs, to garnish

1 Bring a large saucepan of water
to the boil and cook the spaghetti
until 'al dente' or according to the
instructions on the packet. Drain.

2 Place the aubergine, courgette and
pepper on a baking sheet.

3 Mix the oil and garlic together and
spoon over the vegetables, tossing
to coat.

4 Cook under a preheated hot grill
for about 10 minutes, turning, until
tender and lightly charred. Set aside
and keep warm.

5 Divide the spaghetti among 4
lightly greased Yorkshire pudding
tins. Using a fork, curl the spaghetti to
form nests.

6 Brush the pasta nests with melted
butter or margarine and sprinkle with
the breadcrumbs. Bake in a preheated
oven, at 200°C/400°F/ Gas Mark 6, for

15 minutes or until lightly golden.
Remove the pasta nests from the tins
and transfer to serving plates. Divide
the grilled vegetables between the
pasta nests, season and garnish.

COOK'S TIP

'Al dente' means 'to the bite' and
describes cooked pasta that is not too
soft, but still has a bite to it.

Spring Vegetable & Tofu Fusilli

This is a simple, clean-tasting dish of green vegetables,
tofu and pasta, lightly tossed in olive oil.

Serves 4
250 g/9 oz asparagus
125 g/4½ oz mangetout
250 g/9 oz French beans
1 leek
250 g/9 oz shelled small broad beans
300 g/10½ oz dried fusilli
2 tbsp olive oil
25 g/1 oz butter or vegetarian margarine
1 garlic clove, crushed
250 g/9 oz tofu, cut into 2.5 cm/1 inch cubes
60 g/2 oz pitted green olives in brine, drained
salt and pepper
freshly grated Parmesan, to serve

1 Cut the asparagus into 5 cm/2 inch lengths. Finely slice the mangetout diagonally and slice the French beans into 2.5 cm/1 inch pieces. Finely slice the leek.

2 Bring a large saucepan of water to the boil and add the asparagus, green beans and broad beans. Bring back to the boil and cook for 4 minutes until just tender. Drain well and rinse in cold water. Set aside.

3 Bring a large pan of salted water to the boil and cook the fusilli for 8–9 minutes until just tender. Drain well. Toss in 1 tbsp of the oil and season.

4 Meanwhile, in a wok or large frying pan, heat the remaining oil and the butter or margarine and gently fry the leek, garlic and tofu for 1–2 minutes

until the vegetables are softened, but not browned.

5 Stir in the mangetout and cook for 1 minute.

6 Add the boiled vegetables and olives to the pan and heat through for 1 minute. Carefully stir in the pasta and seasoning. Cook for 1 minute and pile into a warmed serving dish. Serve sprinkled with Parmesan.

Fried Noodles with Bean-sprouts, Chives & Chillies

This is a simple idea to jazz up noodles which accompany
main course dishes in Thailand.

Serves 4
500 g/1 lb 2 oz medium egg noodles
60 g/2 oz bean-sprouts
15 g/$^{1}/_{2}$ oz chives
3 tbsp sunflower oil
1 garlic clove, crushed
4 green chillies, deseeded,
sliced and soaked in
2 tbsp rice vinegar
salt

1 To cook the noodles, soak them in boiling water for 10 minutes. Drain and set aside.

2 Soak the bean-sprouts in cold water while you cut the chives into 2.5 cm/1 inch pieces. Set a few chives aside for garnish. Drain the bean-sprouts thoroughly.

3 Heat the oil in a wok or large, heavy frying pan. Add the crushed garlic and stir; then add the chillies and stir until fragrant, about 1 minute.

4 Add the bean-sprouts, stir and then add the noodles. Stir in a little salt and the chives. Using 2 spoons, lift and stir the noodles for 1 minute.

5 Garnish the finished dish with the reserved chives, and serve immediately.

Vegetable-filled Ravioli

These small parcels are very easy to make and have
the advantage of being filled with your favourite mixture of succulent mushrooms.
Serve with freshly grated cheese sprinkled on top.

Serves 4
FILLING
25 g/1 oz butter or
vegetarian margarine
2 garlic cloves, crushed
1 small leek, chopped
2 celery sticks, chopped
200 g/7 oz open-cup mushrooms, chopped
1 egg, beaten
2 tbsp grated Parmesan cheese
salt and pepper
RAVIOLI
4 sheets filo pastry
25 g/1 oz vegetarian margarine
oil, for deep-frying

1 To make the filling, melt the butter
or margarine in a frying pan and sauté
the garlic and leek for 2–3 minutes.
Add the celery and mushrooms and
cook for a further 4–5 minutes until
all of the vegetables are tender.

2 Turn off the heat and stir in the egg
and Parmesan cheese. Season with
salt and pepper to taste.

3 Lay the pastry sheets on a chopping
board and cut each into nine squares.
Spoon a little of the filling into the
centre half of the squares and brush
the edges of the pastry with butter or
margarine. Lay another square on top
and seal the edges to make a parcel.

4 Heat the oil for deep-frying to
180°C/350°F or until a cube of bread
browns in 30 seconds. Fry the ravioli,
in batches, for 2–3 minutes or until

golden brown. Remove from the oil
with a slotted spoon and pat dry on
absorbent kitchen paper. Transfer to a
warm serving plate and serve.

COOK'S TIP

If time is short, boil some frozen mixed
vegetables and use as a quick filling for
the ravioli.

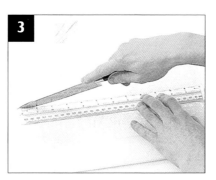

Pasta with Pine Kernels & Blue Cheese

Simple, quick and inexpensive, this tasty pasta dish
can be prepared in minutes.

Serves 4
60 g/2 oz pine kernels
350 g/12 oz dried pasta shapes
2 courgettes, sliced
125 g/4^1/$_2$ oz broccoli, broken into florets
200 g/7 oz full-fat soft cheese
150 ml/^{1}/$_4$ pint milk
1 tbsp chopped fresh basil
125 g/4^1/$_2$ oz button mushrooms, sliced
90 g/3 oz blue cheese, crumbled
salt and pepper
sprigs of fresh basil, to garnish
green salad, to serve

1 Scatter the pine kernels on to a baking sheet and cook under a preheated grill, turning occasionally, until lightly browned all over. Set aside.

2 Cook the pasta in plenty of boiling salted water for 8–10 minutes until just tender. Meanwhile, cook the courgettes and broccoli in a small amount of boiling, lightly salted water for about 5 minutes until tender.

3 Put the soft cheese into a saucepan and heat gently, stirring constantly. Add the milk and stir to mix.

COOK'S TIP

Watch the pine kernels carefully, otherwise they will burn. They will toast in 2–3 minutes.

4 Add the basil and mushrooms and cook gently for 2–3 minutes. Stir in the blue cheese and season to taste.

5 Drain the pasta and the vegetables and mix together. Pour the cheese and mushroom sauce over and add the pine kernels. Toss gently to mix. Garnish with basil sprigs and serve with a green salad.

Vegetable Lasagne

This colourful and tasty lasagne, with layers of vegetables in tomato sauce and aubergines, all topped with a rich cheese sauce is simply delicious.

Serves 4

1 aubergine, sliced

3 tbsp olive oil

2 garlic cloves, crushed

1 red onion, halved and sliced

1 green pepper, diced

1 red pepper, diced

1 yellow pepper, diced

225 g/8 oz mixed mushrooms, sliced

2 celery sticks, sliced

1 courgette, diced

$^1/_2$ tsp chilli powder

$^1/_2$ tsp ground cumin

2 tomatoes, chopped

300 ml/$^1/_2$ pint passata

2 tbsp chopped basil

8 no pre-cook lasagne verdi sheets

CHEESE SAUCE

2 tbsp butter or vegetarian margarine

1 tbsp flour

150 ml/$^1/_4$ pint vegetable stock

300 ml/$^1/_2$ pint milk

75 g/$2^3/_4$ oz Cheddar, grated

1 tsp Dijon mustard

1 tbsp chopped basil

1 egg, beaten

1 Place the aubergine slices in a colander, sprinkle with salt and leave for 20 minutes. Rinse under cold water, drain and reserve. Heat the oil in a pan and sauté the garlic and onion for 1–2 minutes. Add the peppers, mushrooms, celery and courgette and cook for 3–4 minutes, stirring. Stir in the spices and cook for 1 minute. Mix the tomatoes, passata and basil together and season well.

2 For the sauce, melt the butter in a pan, add the flour and cook for 1 minute. Remove from the heat and stir in the stock and milk. Return to the heat and add half of the cheese and the mustard. Boil, stirring, until thickened. Stir in the basil and season. Remove the pan from the heat and stir in the egg. Place half of the lasagne sheets in an ovenproof dish. Top with half of the vegetables, then half of the tomato sauce. Cover with half the aubergines. Repeat and spoon the cheese sauce on top. Sprinkle with cheese and cook in a preheated oven, 180°C/350°F/Gas 4, for 40 minutes.

Pasta Provençale

A Mediterranean mixture of red peppers, garlic and courgettes
cooked in olive oil and tossed with pasta.

Serves 4
3 tbsp olive oil
1 onion, sliced
2 garlic cloves, chopped
3 red peppers, deseeded and cut into strips
3 courgettes, sliced
400 g/14 oz can chopped tomatoes
3 tbsp sun-dried tomato paste
2 tbsp chopped fresh basil
250 g/9 oz fresh pasta spirals
125 g/4¹/₂ oz grated Gruyère cheese
salt and pepper
fresh basil sprigs, to garnish

1 Heat the oil in a heavy-based saucepan or flameproof casserole.

2 Add the onion and garlic and cook, stirring occasionally, until softened.

3 Add the peppers and courgettes and fry for 5 minutes, stirring occasionally.

4 Add the tomatoes, sun-dried tomato paste, basil and salt and pepper to taste, cover and cook for 5 minutes, stirring.

5 Meanwhile, bring a large saucepan of salted water to the boil and add the pasta. Stir and bring back to the boil. Reduce the heat slightly and cook, uncovered, for 3 minutes, or until just tender. Drain the pasta thoroughly.

6 Add the pasta to the vegetables and toss gently to mix well. Put the mixture into a shallow ovenproof dish and sprinkle with the cheese.

7 Cook under a preheated grill for 5 minutes until the cheese is golden brown. Garnish with fresh basil sprigs and serve.

Tagliatelle Tricolore with Broccoli & Cheese Sauce

Some of the simplest and most satisfying dishes are made with pasta,
such as this delicious combination of tagliatelle with its two-cheese sauce.

Serves 4

300 g/10$^{1}/_{2}$ oz dried tagliatelle
tricolore (plain, spinach-and tomato-
flavoured noodles)

250 g/9 oz broccoli, broken into
small florets

350g/12 oz Mascarpone
cheese

125 g/4$^{1}/_{2}$ oz blue cheese,
chopped

1 tbsp chopped fresh oregano

30 g/1 oz butter

salt and pepper

sprigs of fresh oregano, to garnish

freshly grated Parmesan, to serve

1 Cook the tagliatelle in a saucepan of boiling salted water until just tender, according to the instructions on the packet.

2 Meanwhile, cook the broccoli florets in a small amount of lightly salted, boiling water. Avoid overcooking the broccoli, so that it retains its colour and texture.

3 Heat the Mascarpone and blue cheeses together gently in a large saucepan until they are melted.

4 Stir in the oregano and season with salt and pepper to taste.

5 Drain the tagliatelle thoroughly and return to the pan. Add the cheese sauce and butter and toss to coat.

6 Drain the broccoli and add to the pasta, tossing to mix.

7 Divide the pasta between 4 warmed serving plates.

8 Garnish with sprigs of fresh oregano and serve with freshly grated Parmesan cheese.

COOK'S TIP

Choose your favourite pasta shapes as
an alternative to tagliatelle,
if you prefer.

Vegetable Cannelloni

This dish is made with prepared cannelloni tubes,
but may also be made by rolling ready-bought lasagne sheets.

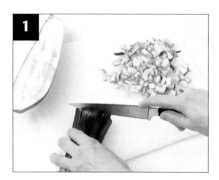

Serves 4
1 aubergine
125 ml/4 fl oz olive oil
225 g/8 oz spinach
2 garlic cloves, crushed
1 tsp ground cumin
75 g/2³⁄₄ oz mushrooms, chopped
12 cannelloni tubes
salt and pepper

TOMATO SAUCE

1 tbsp olive oil
1 onion, chopped
2 garlic cloves, crushed
2 x 400 g/14 oz cans chopped tomatoes
1 tsp caster sugar
2 tbsp chopped basil
50 g/1³⁄₄ oz Mozzarella, sliced

1 Cut the aubergines into small dice.

2 Heat the oil in a frying pan and cook the aubergines for 2–3 minutes.

3 Add the spinach, garlic, cumin, mushrooms and season to taste and cook for 2–3 minutes, stirring. Spoon the mixture into the cannelloni tubes and place in an ovenproof dish in a single layer.

4 To make the sauce, heat the olive oil in a saucepan and sauté the onion and garlic for 1 minute. Add the tomatoes, caster sugar and basil and bring to the boil. Reduce the heat and simmer for 5 minutes. Pour the sauce over the cannelloni tubes.

5 Arrange the sliced Mozzarella on top of the sauce and cook in a preheated oven, 190°C/375°F/Gas Mark 5, for 30 minutes or until the cheese is bubbling and golden brown. Serve immediately.

COOK'S TIP

You can prepare the tomato sauce in advance and store it in the refrigerator for up to 24 hours.

Three-Cheese Macaroni Bake

Based on a traditional family favourite, this pasta bake has plenty of flavour.
Serve with a crisp salad for a quick, tasty supper.

Serves 4
600 ml/1 pint Béchamel Sauce (see page 14)
250 g/9 oz macaroni
1 egg, beaten
125 g/4¹⁄₂ oz grated mature Cheddar
1 tbsp wholegrain mustard
2 tbsp chopped fresh chives
4 tomatoes, sliced
125 g/4¹⁄₂ oz grated Red Leicester cheese
60 g/2 oz grated blue cheese
2 tbsp sunflower seeds
salt and pepper
snipped fresh chives, to garnish

1 Make the béchamel sauce, put into a bowl and cover with cling film to prevent a skin forming. Set aside until required.

2 Bring a saucepan of salted water to the boil and cook the macaroni for 8–10 minutes until just tender. Drain well and place in an ovenproof dish.

3 Stir the beaten egg, Cheddar, mustard, chives and salt and pepper to taste into the béchamel sauce. Spoon the sauce over the macaroni, making sure it is well covered.

4 Arrange a layer of sliced tomatoes on top of the sauce.

5 Sprinkle over the Red Leicester and blue cheeses, and the sunflower seeds.

6 Place on a baking sheet and bake in a preheated oven, 190°C/375°F/Gas Mark 5, for 25–30 minutes until bubbling and golden.

7 Garnish the macaroni bake with freshly snipped chives and serve immediately.

Tagliatelle with Courgette Sauce

This is a really fresh tasting dish which is ideal with a crisp white wine and some crusty bread.

Serves 4
6 tbsp olive oil
3 garlic cloves, crushed
650 g/1 lb 7 oz courgettes
3 tbsp chopped basil
2 red chillies, sliced
juice of 1 large lemon
5 tbsp single cream
4 tbsp grated Parmesan cheese
225 g/8 oz tagliatelle
salt and pepper
chopped basil and lemon zest, to garnish

1 Using a vegetable peeler, slice the courgettes into thin ribbons.

2 Heat the oil in a frying pan and sauté the garlic for 30 seconds. Add the courgettes and cook over a gentle heat, stirring, for 5–7 minutes.

3 Stir in the basil, chilli, lemon juice, cream and Parmesan and season well.

4 Meanwhile, cook the pasta in a large pan of boiling salted water for 10 minutes until 'al dente'. Drain well and put in a warm serving bowl. Pile the courgette mixture on top of the pasta. Garnish with chopped fresh basil and lemon zest and serve immediately.

COOK'S VARIATION

Lime juice and zest could be used instead of the lemon as an alternative.

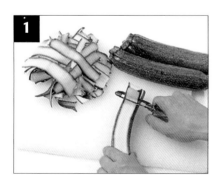

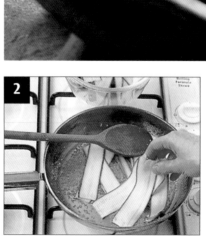

Spaghetti with Pear & Walnut Sauce

This is quite an unusual combination of ingredients in a savoury dish,
but is absolutely wonderful tossed into a fine pasta such as spaghetti.

Serves 4
225 g/8 oz spaghetti
2 small ripe pears, peeled and sliced
150 ml/¼ pint vegetable stock
85 ml/3 fl oz dry white wine
2 tbsp butter
1 tbsp olive oil
1 red onion, quartered and sliced
1 garlic clove, crushed
50 g/1¾ oz walnut halves
2 tbsp chopped oregano
1 tbsp lemon juice
75 g/2¾ oz dolcelatte cheese
salt and pepper
fresh oregano sprigs, to garnish

1 Cook the pasta in a saucepan of boiling salted water for 8–10 minutes or until 'al dente'. Drain thoroughly.

2 Meanwhile, place the pears in a pan and pour over the stock and wine. Poach the pears over a gentle heat for 10 minutes. Drain and reserve the cooking liquid and pears.

3 Melt the butter with the oil and sauté the red onion and garlic for 2–3 minutes, stirring.

4 Add the walnuts, oregano and lemon juice, stirring.

5 Stir in the pears and 4 tablespoons of the poaching liquid.

6 Crumble the dolcelatte cheese into the pan and cook over a gentle heat, stirring occasionally, for 1–2 minutes or until the cheese just begins to melt.

Season the sauce with salt and pepper to taste.

7 Toss the pasta into the sauce, garnish and serve.

COOK'S TIP

You can use any good-flavoured blue cheese for this dish.

Olive, Pepper & Tomato Pasta

The sweet cherry tomatoes in this recipe add colour and flavour
and are complemented by the black olives and peppers.

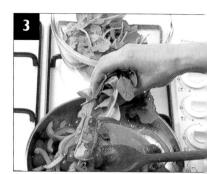

Serves 4
225 g/8 oz penne
2 tbsp olive oil
2 tbsp butter
2 garlic cloves, crushed
1 green pepper, thinly sliced
1 yellow pepper, thinly sliced
16 cherry tomatoes, halved
1 tbsp chopped oregano
125 ml/4 floz dry white wine
2 tbsp quartered, pitted black olives
75 g/2³/₄ oz rocket
salt and pepper
fresh oregano sprigs, to garnish

1 Cook the pasta in a saucepan of
boiling salted water for 8–10 minutes
or until 'al dente'. Drain thoroughly.

2 Heat the oil and butter in a pan
until the butter melts. Sauté the garlic
for 30 seconds. Add the peppers and
cook for 3–4 minutes, stirring.

3 Stir in the cherry tomatoes,
oregano, wine and olives and cook for
3–4 minutes. Season well and stir in
the rocket until just wilted.

4 Transfer the pasta to a serving dish
and spoon the sauce on top. Toss well
to mix, garnish and serve.

COOK'S TIP

Ensure that the saucepan is
large enough to prevent the
pasta from sticking together
during cooking.

Baked Pasta in Tomato Sauce

This pasta dish is baked in a pudding basin and cut into slices for serving.
It looks and tastes terrific and is perfect when you want to impress.

Serves 8

100 g/3¹/₂ oz pasta shapes,
such as penne or casareccia

1 tbsp olive oil

1 leek, chopped

3 garlic cloves, crushed

1 green pepper, chopped

400 g/14 oz can chopped tomatoes

2 tbsp chopped, pitted black olives

2 eggs, beaten

1 tbsp chopped basil

TOMATO SAUCE

1 tbsp olive oil

1 onion, chopped

225 g/8 oz can chopped tomatoes

1 tsp caster sugar

2 tbsp tomato purée

150 ml/¹/₄ pint vegetable stock

salt and pepper

1 Cook the pasta in a saucepan of boiling salted water for 8 minutes. Drain thoroughly.

2 Meanwhile, heat the oil in a saucepan and sauté the leek and garlic for 2 minutes, stirring. Add the pepper, tomatoes and olives and cook for a further 5 minutes.

3 Remove the pan from the heat and stir in the pasta, beaten eggs and basil. Season well, and spoon into a lightly greased 1 litre/2 pint ovenproof pudding basin.

4 Place the pudding basin in a roasting tin and half-fill the tin with boiling water. Cover the tin and cook

in a preheated oven, 180°C/350°F/Gas Mark 6, for 40 minutes until the mixture has set.

5 To make the sauce, heat the oil in a pan and sauté the onion for 2 minutes. Add the remaining ingredients and cook for 10 minutes.

Put the sauce in a food processor or blender and blend until smooth. Return to a clean saucepan and heat until hot.

6 Turn the pasta out of the pudding basin on to a warm plate. Slice and serve with the tomato sauce.

Grains & Pulses

Grains are the seeds of cultivated grasses, while pulses are the dried seeds of pod-bearing plants of the Leguminosae family. Together they are the most universally important staple foods. Grains include wheat, corn, barley, rye, oats, buckwheat and many varieties of rice, as well as associated flours. Pulses include chick-peas, yellow and green split peas, a fascinating variety of beans, together with many types of lentil.

Grains and pulses form a substantial base to which other ingredients can be added. Each has its own distinctive flavour and texture, so it's worth experimenting with less well-known varieties. An excellent source of protein, iron, calcium and B vitamins, these valuable foods are cheap, highly nutritious, versatile and filling, and are virtually fat-free. With the current emphasis on healthier eating, they are a must for the vegetarian diet.

Vegetable Jambalaya

This dish traditionally contains spicy sausage but it is equally delicious filled with vegetables in this spicy vegetarian version.

Serves 4
75 g/2³/₄ oz brown rice
2 tbsp olive oil
2 garlic cloves, crushed
1 red onion, cut into eight
1 aubergine, diced
1 green pepper, diced
50 g/1³/₄ oz baby corn cobs, halved lengthwise
50 g/1³/₄ oz frozen peas
100 g/3¹/₂ oz small broccoli florets
150 ml/5 floz vegetable stock
225 ml/8 fl oz can chopped tomatoes
1 tbsp tomato purée
1 tsp creole seasoning
¹/₂ tsp chilli flakes
salt and pepper

5 Stir the brown rice into the vegetable mixture and cook, mixing well, for 3–4 minutes or until hot.

6 Transfer the vegetable jambalaya to warm serving dishes and serve immediately.

COOK'S TIP

Use a mixture of rice, such as wild or red rice, for colour and texture. Cook the rice in advance for a speedier recipe.

1 Cook the rice in a saucepan of boiling water for 20 minutes or until cooked through. Drain thoroughly and set aside until required.

2 Heat the oil in a heavy-based frying pan and cook the garlic and onion for 2–3 minutes, stirring.

3 Add the aubergine, pepper, corn, peas and broccoli to the pan and cook, stirring occasionally, for 2–3 minutes.

4 Stir in the stock and canned tomatoes, tomato purée, creole seasoning and chilli flakes. Season with salt and pepper to taste and cook over a low heat for 15–20 minutes or until the vegetables are tender.

Mushroom & Parmesan Risotto

Make this creamy risotto with Italian arborio rice
and freshly grated Parmesan for the best results.

Serves 4

2 tbsp olive or vegetable oil

250 g/9 oz
arborio rice

2 garlic cloves, crushed

1 onion, chopped

2 celery stalks, chopped

1 red or green pepper,
deseeded and chopped

250 g/9 oz mushrooms,
sliced

1 tbsp chopped fresh oregano
or 1 tsp dried oregano

1 litre/1¾ pints Fresh
Vegetable Stock (see page 14)

60 g/2 oz sun-dried
tomatoes in olive oil,
drained and chopped (optional)

60 g/2 oz freshly
grated Parmesan

salt and pepper

TO GARNISH

fresh flat-leaf parsley sprigs
fresh bay leaves

1 Heat the oil in a wok or large frying pan. Add the rice and cook, stirring, for 5 minutes.

2 Add the garlic, onion, celery and pepper and cook, stirring, for 5 minutes. Add the mushrooms and cook for a further 3–4 minutes.

3 Stir in the oregano and stock. Heat until just boiling, then reduce the heat, cover and simmer gently for about 20 minutes until the rice is tender and creamy.

4 Add the sun-dried tomatoes, if using, and season with salt and pepper to taste. Stir in half the Parmesan. Top with the remaining cheese, and garnish with flat-leaf parsley and bay leaves. Serve.

COOK'S TIP

Add the stock a little at a time, only adding more when the last addition is fully absorbed.

Oriental-style Millet Pilau

Millet makes an interesting alternative to rice, which is the more traditional ingredient for a pilau. Serve with a crisp salad of oriental vegetables.

Serves 4
300 g/10¹/₂ oz millet grains
1 tbsp vegetable oil
1 bunch spring onions, white and green parts, chopped
1 garlic clove, crushed
1 tsp grated ginger root
1 orange pepper, deseeded and diced
600 ml/1 pint water
1 orange
125 g/4¹/₂ oz chopped pitted dates
2 tsp sesame oil
125 g/4¹/₂ oz roasted cashew nuts
2 tbsp pumpkin seeds
salt and pepper
oriental salad vegetables, to serve

1 Place the millet in a large saucepan and cook over a medium heat for 4–5 minutes to toast, shaking the pan occasionally, until the grains begin to crack and pop.

2 Heat the oil in a separate saucepan and gently fry the spring onions, garlic, ginger and pepper for 2–3 minutes until just softened but not browned. Add the millet and pour in the water.

3 Using a vegetable peeler, pare the rind from the orange and add the rind to the pan. Squeeze the juice from the orange into the pan. Season well.

4 Bring the mixture to the boil, reduce the heat, cover and cook gently for 20 minutes or until all of the liquid has been absorbed. Remove the pan from the heat, stir in the dates and sesame oil and leave to stand for 10 minutes.

5 Discard the orange rind and stir in the cashew nuts. Transfer to a serving dish, sprinkle with pumpkin seeds and serve with oriental salad vegetables.

Brown Rice, Vegetable & Herb Gratin

This is a really filling dish and therefore does not require an accompaniment.
It is very versatile, and could be made with a wide selection of vegetables.

Serves 4

100 g/3½ oz brown rice

2 tbsp butter or margarine

1 red onion, chopped

2 garlic cloves, crushed

1 carrot, cut into matchsticks

1 courgette, sliced

75 g/2¾ oz baby corn cobs,
halved lengthwise

2 tbsp sunflower seeds

3 tbsp chopped mixed herbs

100 g/3½ oz grated Mozzarella cheese

2 tbsp wholemeal breadcrumbs

salt and pepper

1 Cook the rice in a saucepan of boiling salted water for 20 minutes or until cooked. Drain well.

2 Lightly grease a 900 ml/1½ pint ovenproof dish.

3 Heat the butter in a frying pan. Add the onion and cook, stirring, for 2 minutes or until softened.

4 Add the garlic, carrot, courgette and corn cobs and cook for a further 5 minutes, stirring.

5 Mix the rice with the sunflower seeds and mixed herbs and stir into the pan.

6 Stir in half of the Mozzarella cheese and season with salt and pepper to taste.

7 Spoon the mixture into the greased dish and top with the breadcrumbs and remaining cheese. Cook in a preheated oven, 180°C/350°F/Gas Mark 4, for 25–30 minutes or until the cheese begins to turn golden. Serve.

COOK'S VARIATION

Use an alternative rice, such as basmati, and flavour the dish with curry spices, if you prefer.

Chatuchak Fried Rice

An excellent way to use up leftover rice. Pop it into the freezer
as soon as it is cool, and it will be ready to reheat at any time.

Serves 4

1 tbsp sunflower oil

2 garlic cloves, crushed

2.5 cm/1 inch piece ginger root,
shredded finely

3 shallots, chopped finely

1 red chilli, deseeded
and chopped finely

$^1\!/_2$ green pepper, deseeded
and sliced finely

150 g/5$^1\!/_2$ oz baby aubergines,
quartered

90 g/3 oz sugar snap peas
or mangetout,
trimmed and blanched

90 g/3 oz baby corn cobs, halved
lengthwise and blanched

1 tomato, cut into 8 pieces

90 g/3 oz bean-sprouts

500 g/1 lb 2 oz cooked
Thai jasmine rice

2 tbsp tomato ketchup

2 tbsp light soy sauce

TO GARNISH

fresh coriander leaves

lime wedges

1 Heat the sunflower oil in a wok or
large, heavy frying pan over a high
heat. Add the garlic and ginger,
stirring well.

2 Add the shallots, chilli, green
pepper and baby aubergines and cook,
stirring, until the shallots have
softened. Add the sugar snap peas or
mangetout, corn cobs, tomato and
bean-sprouts and cook, stirring,
for 3 minutes.

3 Add the rice, and lift and mix with
two spoons for 4–5 minutes, until no
more steam is released. Stir in the
tomato ketchup and soy sauce.

4 Transfer to serving dishes and serve
immediately, garnished with coriander
leaves and lime wedges to squeeze
over the rice.

Green Lentil &
Mixed Vegetable Pan-fry

The green lentils used in this recipe require soaking but are worth it for the flavour.
If time is short, use red split peas which do not require soaking.

Serves 4

150 g/5½ oz green lentils
4 tbsp butter or vegetarian margarine
2 garlic cloves, crushed
2 tbsp olive oil
1 tbsp cider vinegar
1 red onion, cut into eight
50 g/1¾ oz baby corn cobs, halved lengthwise
1 yellow pepper, cut into strips
1 red pepper, cut into strips
50 g/1¾ oz French beans, halved
125 ml/4 fl oz vegetable stock
2 tbsp clear honey
salt and pepper

1 Soak the lentils in a large saucepan of cold water for 25 minutes. Bring to the boil, reduce the heat and simmer for 20 minutes. Drain thoroughly.

2 Add 1 tablespoon of the butter or margarine, 1 garlic clove, 1 tablespoon of oil and the vinegar to the lentils and mix well.

3 Melt the remaining butter and oil in a frying pan and stir-fry the onion, corn cobs, pepper and beans for 3–4 minutes.

4 Add the stock and bring to the boil for about 10 minutes or until the liquid has evaporated.

5 Add the honey and season with salt and pepper to taste. Stir in the lentil mixture and cook for 1 minute to heat through. Spoon on to warmed serving plates and serve with crusty bread.

Chick-pea & Peanut Balls

These tasty, nutty morsels are delicious served with a fiery,
tangy sauce that counteracts the richness of the peanuts.

Serves 4
3 tbsp groundnut oil
1 onion, chopped finely
1 celery stalk, chopped
1 tsp dried mixed herbs
250 g/9 oz roasted unsalted peanuts, ground
175 g/6 oz canned chick-peas, drained and mashed
1 tsp yeast extract
60 g/2 oz fresh wholemeal breadcrumbs
1 egg yolk
30 g/1 oz plain flour
strips of fresh red chilli, to garnish
boiled rice and green salad leaves, to serve

HOT CHILLI SAUCE

2 tsp groundnut oil
1 large red chilli, deseeded and chopped finely
2 spring onions, chopped finely
2 tbsp red wine vinegar
200 g/7 oz can chopped tomatoes
2 tbsp tomato purée
2 tsp caster sugar
salt and pepper

1 Heat 1 tablespoon of the oil in a frying pan and gently fry the onion and celery for 3–4 minutes until softened but not browned.

2 Place all the other ingredients, except for the remaining oil and the flour, in a mixing bowl and add the onion and celery. Mix well.

3 Divide the mixture into 12 portions and roll into balls. Coat with the flour.

4 Heat the remaining oil in a frying pan. Add the chick-pea balls and cook over a medium heat for 15 minutes, turning frequently, until cooked through and golden. Drain on paper towels.

5 Meanwhile, make the hot chilli sauce. Heat the oil in a small frying

pan and gently fry the chilli and spring onions for 2–3 minutes. Stir in the remaining ingredients and season. Bring to the boil and simmer for 5 minutes.

6 Serve the chick-pea and peanut balls with the hot chilli sauce, rice and a green salad.

Cashew Nut Paella

Paella traditionally contains chicken and fish, but this recipe is packed with vegetables and nuts for a truly delicious and simple vegetarian dish.

Serves 4
2 tbsp olive oil
1 tbsp butter
1 red onion, chopped
150 g/5^1/$_2$ oz arborio rice
1 tsp ground turmeric
1 tsp ground cumin
^{1}/$_2$ tsp chilli powder
3 garlic cloves, crushed
1 green chilli, sliced
1 green pepper, diced
1 red pepper, diced
75 g/2^3/$_4$ oz baby corn cobs, halved lengthwise
2 tbsp pitted black olives
1 large tomato, seeded and diced
450 ml/^{3}/$_4$ pint vegetable stock
75 g/2^3/$_4$ oz unsalted cashew nuts
25 g/1 oz frozen peas
2 tbsp chopped parsley
pinch of cayenne pepper
salt and pepper
fresh herbs, to garnish

1 Heat the oil and butter in a large frying pan or paella pan until the butter has melted.

2 Add the onion to the pan and sauté for 2–3 minutes, stirring.

3 Stir in the rice, turmeric, cumin, chilli powder, garlic, chilli, peppers, corn cobs, olives and tomato and cook over a medium heat for 1–2 minutes, stirring.

4 Pour in the stock and bring the mixture to the boil. Reduce the heat and cook for 20 minutes, stirring.

5 Add the cashew nuts and peas to the mixture in the pan and cook for a further 5 minutes, stirring occasionally. Season with salt and pepper to taste and sprinkle with parsley and cayenne pepper. Transfer to warm serving plates, garnish and serve immediately.

COOK'S TIP

For authenticity and flavour, use a few saffron strands soaked in a little boiling water instead of the turmeric. Saffron has a lovely, nutty flavour.

Cheesy Semolina Fritters with Apple Relish

Based on a gnocchi recipe, these delicious fritters are
accompanied by a fruity home-made relish.

Serves 4
600 ml/1 pint milk
1 small onion
1 celery stalk
1 bay leaf
2 cloves
125 g/4^1/$_2$ oz semolina
125 g/4^1/$_2$ oz grated mature Cheddar
^{1}/$_2$ tsp dried mustard powder
2 tbsp plain flour
1 egg, beaten
60 g/2 oz dried white breadcrumbs
6 tbsp vegetable oil
salt and pepper
celery leaves, to garnish
coleslaw, to serve

RELISH
2 celery stalks, chopped
2 small dessert apples, cored and diced finely
90 g/3 oz sultanas
90 g/3 oz no-soak dried apricots, chopped
6 tbsp cider vinegar
pinch of ground cloves
^{1}/$_2$ tsp ground cinnamon

1 Pour the milk into a pan and add the onion, celery, bay leaf and cloves. Bring to the boil, remove from the heat and let stand for 15 minutes.

2 Strain the mixture into another pan, bring to the boil and sprinkle in the semolina, stirring constantly. Reduce the heat and simmer for 5 minutes until very thick, stirring occasionally to prevent it sticking.

3 Remove from the heat and beat in the cheese, mustard and seasoning. Place in a greased bowl and let cool.

4 To make the relish, put all of the ingredients in a pan, bring to the boil, cover and simmer for 20 minutes, until tender. Let cool.

5 Put the flour, egg and breadcrumbs on to separate plates. Divide the cooled semolina mixture into eight and press into 6 cm/2½ inch rounds. Coat the rounds lightly in the flour, then in the egg and breadcrumbs. Heat the oil in a large frying pan and fry the fritters for 3–4 minutes on each side until golden. Drain on paper towels. Garnish and serve with the relish and coleslaw.

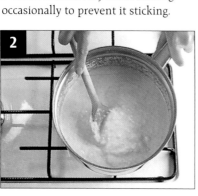

Pesto Rice with Garlic Bread

Try this combination of two types of rice with the richness
of pine kernels, basil, and freshly grated Parmesan.

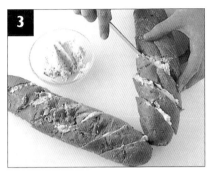

Serves 4

300 g/10½ oz mixed
long-grain and wild rice
fresh basil sprigs, to garnish
tomato and orange salad, to serve

PESTO DRESSING

15 g/½ oz fresh basil leaves
125 g/4½ oz pine kernels
2 garlic cloves, crushed
6 tbsp olive oil
60 g/2 oz freshly
grated Parmesan
salt and pepper

GARLIC BREAD

2 small granary or wholemeal
French bread sticks
90 g/3 oz butter or
vegetarian margarine, softened
2 garlic cloves, crushed
1 tsp dried mixed herbs

1 Place the rice in a saucepan and
cover with water. Bring to the boil and
cook according to the packet
instructions. Drain thoroughly, set
aside and keep warm.

2 Meanwhile, make the pesto
dressing. Remove the basil leaves
from the stalks and finely chop the
leaves. Reserve 30 g/1 oz of the pine
kernels and finely chop the
remainder. Mix with the chopped
basil and the rest of the dressing
ingredients. Alternatively, put all of
the ingredients in a food processor or
blender and blend for a few seconds
until smooth. Set aside.

3 To make the garlic bread, slice the
bread at 2.5 cm/1 inch intervals,
taking care not to slice all the way
through. Mix the butter or margarine
with the garlic, herbs and seasoning.
Spread thickly between each slice.

4 Wrap the bread in foil and bake in a
preheated oven, 200°C/400°F/Gas
Mark 6, for 10–15 minutes.

5 To serve, toast the reserved pine
kernels under a preheated medium
grill for 2–3 minutes until golden. Toss
the pesto dressing into the hot rice
and transfer to a warm serving dish.
Sprinkle with toasted pine kernels and
garnish with basil sprigs. Serve with
the garlic bread and a tomato and
orange salad.

Lentil & Rice Casserole

This is a really hearty dish, perfect for cold days
when a filling hot dish is just what you need.

Serves 4
225 g/8 oz red split lentils
50 g/1¾ oz long-grain white rice
1 litre/1¾ pints vegetable stock
150 ml/¼ pint dry white wine
1 leek, cut into chunks
3 garlic cloves, crushed
400 g/14 oz can chopped tomatoes
1 tsp ground cumin
1 tsp chilli powder
1 tsp garam masala
1 red pepper, sliced
100 g/3½ oz small broccoli florets
8 baby corn cobs, halved lengthwise
50 g/1¾ oz French beans, halved
1 tbsp fresh basil, shredded
fresh basil sprigs, to garnish

1 Place the lentils, rice, stock and
wine in a flameproof casserole dish
and cook over a gentle heat for 20
minutes, stirring occasionally.

2 Add the leek, garlic, tomatoes,
spices, pepper, broccoli, corn cobs and
beans. Bring the mixture to the boil,
reduce the heat, cover and simmer for
a further 10–15 minutes or until the
vegetables are tender. Add the
shredded basil and season to taste.
Garnish with fresh basil sprigs and
serve immediately.

COOK'S VARIATION

You can vary the rice in this recipe –
use brown or wild rice, if
you prefer.

Couscous Royale

Serve this stunning dish as a centrepiece for a Moroccan-style feast;
a truly memorable meal.

Serves 4
3 carrots
3 courgettes
350 g/12 oz pumpkin or squash
1.25 litres/2¼ pints Fresh Vegetable Stock (see page 14)
2 cinnamon sticks, broken in half
2 tsp ground cumin
1 tsp ground coriander
pinch of saffron strands
2 tbsp olive oil
pared rind and juice of 1 lemon
2 tbsp clear honey
500 g/1 lb 2 oz pre-cooked couscous
60 g/2 oz butter or vegetarian margarine, softened
175 g/6 oz large seedless raisins
salt and pepper
fresh coriander, to garnish

1 Cut the carrots and courgettes into 7 cm/3 inch pieces and cut in half lengthwise.

2 Trim the pumpkin or squash and discard the seeds. Peel and cut into 7 cm/3 inch pieces.

3 Put the stock, spices, saffron and carrots in a large pan. Bring to the boil, skim off any scum and add the oil. Simmer for 15 minutes. Add the lemon rind and juice to the pan with the honey, courgettes and pumpkin or squash. Season. Bring back to the boil and simmer for 10 minutes.

4 Soak the couscous according to the packet instructions. Transfer to a steamer or large sieve lined with muslin and place over the vegetable pan. Cover and steam as directed. Stir in the butter.

5 Transfer the couscous to a serving plate. Drain the vegetables, reserving the stock, lemon rind and cinnamon. Arrange the vegetables on top of the couscous. Sprinkle the raisins on top and spoon over 6 tbsp of the reserved stock. Keep warm. Return the remaining stock to the heat and boil for 5 minutes to reduce slightly. Discard the lemon rind and cinnamon. Garnish and serve with the sauce.

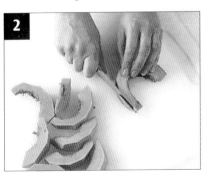

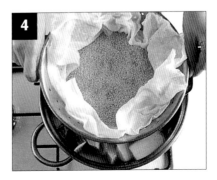

Vegetable Biryani

The Biryani originated in the North of India, and was a dish reserved for festivals.
The main ingredient, the vegetables, are marinated in a yogurt-based marinade and
cooked in a casserole dish with the rice and onions.

Serves 4
1 large potato, cubed
100 g/3½ oz baby carrots
50 g/1¾ oz okra, thickly sliced
2 celery sticks, sliced
75 g/2¾ oz baby button mushrooms, halved
1 aubergine, halved and sliced
300 ml/½ pint natural yogurt
1 tbsp grated root ginger
2 large onions, grated
4 garlic cloves, crushed
1 tsp turmeric
1 tbsp curry powder
2 tbsp butter
2 onions, sliced
225 g/8 oz basmati rice
chopped coriander, to garnish

1 Cook the potato cubes, carrots and okra in a pan of boiling salted water for 7–8 minutes. Drain well and place in a large bowl. Mix with the celery, mushrooms and aubergine.

2 Mix the yogurt, ginger, grated onions, garlic, turmeric and curry powder and pour over the vegetables. Leave to marinate for at least 2 hours.

3 Heat the butter in a frying pan and cook the sliced onions for 5–6 minutes until golden brown. Remove a few onions from the pan and reserve for garnishing.

4 Cook the rice in a pan of boiling water for 7 minutes. Drain well.

5 Add the marinated vegetables to the onions and cook for 10 minutes.

6 Put half of the rice in a 2 litre/3½ pint casserole dish. Spoon the vegetables on top and cover with the remaining rice. Cover and cook in a preheated oven, 190°C/375°F/Gas Mark 5, for 20–25 minutes or until the rice is tender.

7 Spoon the biryani on to a serving plate, garnish with the reserved onions and chopped coriander and serve immediately.

COOK'S VARIATION

Long-grain white rice or brown rice may be used instead of the basmati rice, if you prefer.

Chick-pea & Vegetable Casserole

Serve this hearty dish with warm crusty bread to mop up the juices.

Serves 4
1 tbsp olive oil
1 red onion, halved and sliced
3 garlic cloves, crushed
225 g/8 oz spinach
1 fennel bulb, cut into eight
1 red pepper, cubed
1 tbsp plain flour
450 ml/$^3/_4$ pint vegetable stock
85 ml/3 fl oz dry white wine
400 g/14 oz can chick-peas, drained
1 bay leaf
1 tsp ground coriander
$^1/_2$ tsp paprika
salt and pepper
fennel fronds, to garnish

1 Heat the oil in a large flameproof casserole dish and sauté the onion and garlic for 1 minute, stirring. Add the spinach and cook for 4 minutes or until wilted.

2 Add the fennel and pepper and cook for 2 minutes, stirring. Stir in the flour and cook for 1 minute.

3 Add the stock, wine, chick-peas, bay leaf, coriander and paprika, cover and cook for 30 minutes. Season to taste, garnish with fennel fronds and serve immediately.

COOK'S TIP

Use other canned pulses or mixed beans instead of the chick-peas, if you prefer.

Deep South Spiced Rice & Beans

Cajun spices add a flavour of the American Deep South
to this colourful rice and red kidney bean salad.

Serves 4
175 g/6 oz long-grain rice
4 tbsp olive oil
1 small green pepper, deseeded and chopped
1 small red pepper, deseeded and chopped
1 onion, chopped finely
1 small red or green chilli, deseeded and chopped finely
2 tomatoes, chopped
125 g/4½ oz canned red kidney beans, rinsed and drained
1 tbsp chopped fresh basil
2 tsp chopped fresh thyme (or 1 tsp dried)
1 tsp Cajun spice
salt and pepper
fresh basil leaves and thyme sprigs, to garnish

1 Cook the rice in a saucepan of boiling, lightly salted water for 12 minutes, or until tender. Rinse with cold water and drain well. Transfer to a large bowl.

2 Meanwhile, heat the olive oil in a frying pan. Add the green and red peppers and the onion and cook gently for about 5 minutes, or until softened.

3 Add the chilli and tomatoes, and cook for a further 2 minutes.

4 Add the vegetable mixture and red kidney beans to the rice. Stir well to combine thoroughly.

5 Stir the chopped herbs and Cajun spice into the rice mixture and season with salt and pepper to taste. Transfer to serving plates, garnish with basil leaves and thyme sprigs and serve.

COOK'S TIP

The fresh red or green chilli can be replaced by 1 tsp chilli powder.

Vegetable Curry

Vegetables are cooked in a mildly spiced curry sauce with yogurt
and fresh coriander stirred in just before serving.

Serves 4

2 tbsp sunflower oil

1 onion, sliced

2 tsp cumin seeds

2 tbsp ground coriander

1 tsp ground turmeric

2 tsp ground ginger

1 tsp chopped fresh red chilli

2 garlic cloves, chopped

400 g/14 oz can chopped tomatoes

3 tbsp powdered coconut mixed with
300 ml/^{1}/$_2$ pint boiling water

1 small cauliflower, broken into florets

2 courgettes, sliced

2 carrots, sliced

1 potato, diced

400 g/14 oz can chick-peas,
drained and rinsed

150 ml/^{1}/$_4$ pint thick natural yogurt

2 tbsp mango chutney

3 tbsp chopped fresh coriander

salt and pepper

fresh coriander sprigs, to garnish

MINT RAITA

150 ml/^{1}/$_4$ pint natural yogurt

1 tbsp chopped fresh mint

TO SERVE

onion relish

basmati rice

naan bread

1 Heat the oil in a pan and fry the onion until softened. Add the cumin, ground coriander, turmeric, ginger, chilli and garlic and fry for 1 minute.

2 Add the tomatoes and coconut mixture and mix well.

3 Add the cauliflower, courgettes, carrots, potato, chick-peas and seasoning. Cover and simmer for 20 minutes.

4 Stir in the yogurt, mango chutney and fresh coriander and heat through gently, but do not boil.

5 To make the mint raita, mix the yogurt and mint. Transfer to a serving dish, then cover and chill.

6 Transfer the curry to serving plates, garnish with coriander sprigs and serve with onion relish, mint raita, basmati rice and naan bread.

Egg & Chick-pea Curry

This easy vegetarian curry is always enjoyed. Double the quantities
for a great dish if you're cooking for a crowd.

Serves 4
2 tbsp vegetable oil
2 garlic cloves, crushed
1 large onion, chopped
1 large carrot, sliced
1 apple, cored and chopped
2 tbsp medium-hot curry powder
1 tsp finely grated ginger root
2 tsp paprika
900 ml/1$\frac{1}{2}$ pints Fresh Vegetable Stock (see page 14)
2 tbsp tomato purée
$\frac{1}{2}$ small cauliflower, broken into florets
475 g/1 ib 1 oz can chick-peas, rinsed and drained
25 g/1 oz/2 tbsp sultanas or raisins
2 tbsp cornflour
2 tbsp water
4 hard-boiled eggs, quartered
salt and pepper
paprika, to garnish

CUCUMBER DIP

7.5 cm/3 inch piece cucumber, chopped finely
1 tbsp chopped fresh mint
150 ml/$\frac{1}{4}$ pint natural yogurt
sprigs of fresh mint, to garnish

1 Heat the oil in a large pan and fry
the garlic, onion, carrot and apple for
4–5 minutes, until softened. Add the
curry powder, ginger and paprika and
fry for 1 minute. Stir in the vegetable
stock and tomato purée.

2 Add the cauliflower, chick-peas and
sultanas or raisins. Bring to the boil,
reduce the heat and simmer, covered,
for 25–30 minutes or until tender.

3 Blend the cornflour with the water
and add to the curry, stirring until
thickened. Cook gently for 2 minutes.
Season to taste.

4 To make the dip, mix together the
cucumber, mint and yogurt. Garnish
with fresh mint.

5 Ladle the curry on to 4 serving
plates. Arrange the eggs on top and
sprinkle with a little paprika. Serve
with the cucumber dip.

Risotto Verde

Risotto is an Italian dish which is easy to make and uses arborio rice,
onion and garlic as a base for a range of savoury recipes.

Serves 4
1.75 litres/3 pints vegetable stock
2 tbsp olive oil
2 garlic cloves, crushed
2 leeks, shredded
225 g/8 oz arborio rice
300 ml/$\frac{1}{2}$ pint dry white wine
4 tbsp mixed chopped herbs
225 g/8 oz baby spinach
3 tbsp natural yogurt
shredded leek, to garnish

1 Pour the stock into a large pan and
bring to the boil. Reduce the heat to a
simmer. Meanwhile, heat the oil in a
separate pan and sauté the garlic and
leeks for 2–3 minutes until softened.

2 Stir in the rice and cook for 2
minutes, stirring until well coated.

3 Pour in half of the wine and a little
of the hot stock. Cook over a gentle
heat until all of the liquid has been
absorbed. Add the remaining stock
and cook over a low heat for about 25
minutes or until the rice is creamy.

4 Stir in the herbs and spinach,
season well and cook for 2 minutes.
Stir in the yogurt, garnish and serve.

COOK'S TIP

Do not hurry the process of cooking the
risotto as the rice must absorb the
liquid slowly in order for it to reach the
correct consistency.

Fried Rice In Pineapple

This has a mild, pleasant flavour and looks very impressive
as part of a party buffet, so everyone can enjoy it.

Serves 4-6

1 large pineapple

1 tbsp sunflower oil

1 garlic clove, crushed

1 small onion, diced

$^1/_2$ celery stalk, sliced

1 tsp coriander seeds, ground

1 tsp cumin seeds, ground

150 g/5$^1/_2$ oz button
mushrooms, sliced

250 g/9 oz cooked rice

2 tbsp light soy sauce

$^1/_2$ tsp sugar

$^1/_2$ tsp salt

30 g/1 oz/$^1/_4$ cup cashew nuts

TO GARNISH

1 spring onion,
sliced finely

fresh coriander
leaves

fresh mint sprig

1 Cut the pineapple in half lengthwise and scoop out the flesh to make 2 boat-shaped shells. Cut the flesh into cubes and reserve 125 g/ 4$^1/_2$ oz to use in this recipe. (Any remaining pineapple cubes can be served separately.)

2 Heat the oil in a wok or large, heavy frying pan.

3 Add the garlic, onion and celery and cook over a high heat, stirring constantly, for 2 minutes.

4 Stir in the coriander and cumin seeds, and the mushrooms.

5 Add the pineapple cubes and cooked rice to the pan and stir well. Stir in the soy sauce, sugar, salt and cashew nuts.

6 Using two spoons, lift and stir the

rice for about 4 minutes until it is thoroughly heated through.

7 Spoon the rice mixture into the pineapple boats. Garnish and serve immediately.

Indonesian Hot Rice Salad

Nutty brown rice combines well with peanuts and a sweet and sour mixture
of fruit and vegetables in this tangy combination.

Serves 4

300 g/10½ oz brown rice

400 g/14 oz can pineapple pieces
in natural juice, drained

1 bunch spring onions, chopped

1 red pepper,
deseeded and chopped

125 g/4½ oz bean-sprouts

90 g/3 oz
dry-roasted peanuts

125 g/4½ oz radishes, sliced thinly

DRESSING

2 tbsp crunchy peanut butter

1 tbsp groundnut oil

2 tbsp light soy sauce

2 tbsp white wine vinegar

2 tsp clear honey

1 tsp chilli powder

½ tsp garlic salt

pepper

1 Put the rice in a saucepan and cover with water. Bring to the boil, then cover and simmer for 30 minutes until the rice is tender.

2 Meanwhile, make the dressing. Place all of the ingredients in a small bowl and whisk for a few seconds until well combined.

3 Drain the rice and place in a heatproof bowl. Heat the dressing in a small saucepan for 1 minute and then toss into the rice and mix well.

4 Working quickly, stir in the pineapple, spring onions, pepper, bean-sprouts and peanuts.

5 Transfer the rice salad to a warmed serving dish. Arrange the radish slices around the outside and serve immediately.

COOK'S TIP

Peanut butter is nutritious and can be used to flavour and thicken a wide range of sauces and dressings.

Stir-fries & Sautés

Whether you're cooking a Chinese-style meal or any other kind of dish, stir-frying is one of the most convenient and nutritious ways of cooking vegetarian food. The food is cooked quickly over very high heat in a very little oil. The high heat seals in the natural juices and helps preserve nutrients. The short cooking time makes the vegetables more succulent and preserves texture as well as the natural flavour and colour.

A round-bottomed wok is ideal for stir-frying as it conducts and retains heat evenly. The conical shape requires far less oil and the food always returns to the centre where the heat is most intense, however vigorously you stir.

Sautéeing requires a flat-bottomed pan so that the food can be tossed and stirred without being too crowded. A brisk heat is essential so that the food turns golden and crisp. If you use a non-stick pan you can cut down on the amount of oil required.

Tofu & Vegetable Stir-Fry

This is a quick dish to prepare, making it ideal as a mid-week supper dish,
after a busy day at work!

Serves 4

175 g/6 oz potatoes, cubed
1 tbsp olive oil
1 red onion, sliced
225 g/8 oz firm tofu, diced
2 courgettes, diced
8 canned artichoke hearts, halved
150 ml/$^1/_4$ pint passata
1 tsp caster sugar
2 tbsp chopped basil
salt and pepper

1 Cook the potatoes in a saucepan of boiling water for 10 minutes. Drain thoroughly.

2 Heat the oil in a large frying pan and sauté the red onion for 2 minutes, stirring.

3 Stir in the tofu and courgettes and cook for 3–4 minutes until they begin to brown slightly. Add the potatoes, stirring to mix.

4 Stir in the artichoke hearts, passata, sugar and basil, season with salt and pepper and cook for a further 5 minutes, stirring well. Transfer to serving dishes and serve immediately.

COOK'S VARIATION

Aubergines could be used instead of the courgettes, if preferred.

Red Curry with Cashew Nuts

This is a wonderfully quick dish to prepare. If you don't have time to prepare the curry paste, it can be bought ready-made (use 3 tablespoons for this recipe).

Serves 4

250 ml/9 fl oz coconut milk

1 kaffir lime leaf, mid-rib removed

$1/4$ tsp light soy sauce

60 g/2 oz/4 baby corn cobs, halved lengthwise

125 g/$4^1/_2$ oz broccoli florets

125 g/$4^1/_2$ oz French beans, cut into 5 cm/2 inch pieces

25 g/1 oz cashew nuts

15 fresh basil leaves

1 tbsp chopped fresh coriander

1 tbsp chopped roasted peanuts, to garnish

cooked rice, to serve

RED CURRY PASTE

7 fresh red chillies, halved, deseeded and blanched (use dried if fresh are not available)

2 tsp cumin seeds

2 tsp coriander seeds

2.5 cm/1 inch piece galangal, peeled and chopped

$1/2$ stalk lemon grass, chopped

1 tsp salt

grated rind of 1 lime

4 garlic cloves, chopped

3 shallots, chopped

2 kaffir lime leaves, mid-rib removed, shredded

1 tbsp oil to blend

1 To make the red curry paste, grind the chillies, cumin, coriander, galangal, lemon grass, salt, lime, garlic, shallots and lime leaves in a pestle and mortar, food processor or grinder. Blend with the oil. The paste will keep for up to 3 weeks in a sealed jar in the refrigerator.

2 Preheat a wok or large, heavy frying pan, add 3 tablespoons of the red curry paste and cook over a high heat, stirring, until fragrant.

3 Reduce the heat and add the coconut milk, lime leaf, light soy sauce, corn cobs, broccoli, beans and cashew nuts. Bring to the boil and simmer for about 10 minutes until the vegetables are cooked, but still firm.

4 Remove the lime leaf and stir in the basil leaves and coriander. Garnish with peanuts and serve with the cooked rice.

Three Mushrooms in Coconut Milk

A filling and tasty main course dish served over rice or noodles.

Serves 4
2 lemon grass stalks, sliced thinly
2 green chillies, deseeded and chopped finely
1 tbsp light soy sauce
2 garlic cloves, crushed
2 tbsp chopped fresh coriander
2 tbsp chopped fresh parsley
6 slices galangal, peeled
3 tbsp sunflower oil
1 aubergine, cubed
60 g/2 oz oyster mushrooms
60 g/2 oz chestnut mushrooms
60 g/2 oz field mushrooms, quartered if large
125 g/4$^{1}/_{2}$ oz French beans, cut into 5 cm/2 inch lengths, blanched
300 ml/$^{1}/_{2}$ pint coconut milk
1 tbsp lemon juice
2 tbsp chopped roasted peanuts, to garnish
cooked rice, to serve

1 Grind the lemon grass, chillies, soy sauce, garlic, coriander, parsley and galangal in a large pestle and mortar or a food processor. Set aside until required.

2 Heat the sunflower oil in a preheated wok or large, heavy frying pan. Add the aubergine and stir over a high heat for 3 minutes. Stir in the mushrooms and beans and cook for 3 minutes, stirring constantly. Add the ground spice paste, stirring to mix.

3 Add the coconut milk and lemon juice to the pan, bring the mixture to the boil and simmer for 2 minutes.

4 Serve immediately with rice, and garnish with the roasted peanuts.

Cantonese Garden Vegetable Stir-Fry

This dish tastes as fresh as it looks. Try to get hold of baby vegetables as
they look and taste so much better in this dish.

Serves 4
2 tbsp peanut oil
1 tsp Chinese five spice powder
75 g/2³/₄ oz baby carrots, halved
2 celery sticks, sliced
2 baby leeks, sliced
50 g/1³/₄ oz mangetout
4 baby courgettes, halved lengthwise
8 baby corn cobs
225 g/8 oz firm marinated tofu, cubed
4 tbsp fresh orange juice
1 tbsp clear honey
celery leaves and orange zest, to garnish
cooked rice or noodles, to serve

1 Heat the oil in a preheated wok
until almost smoking. Add the
Chinese five spice powder, carrots,
celery, leeks, mangetout, courgettes
and corn cobs and stir-fry for 3–4
minutes.

2 Add the tofu and cook for a further
2 minutes, stirring.

3 Stir in the orange juice and honey,
reduce the heat and cook for 1–2
minutes. Garnish with celery leaves
and orange zest and serve with rice
or noodles.

COOK'S VARIATION

Lemon juice would be just as delicious
as the orange juice in
this recipe, but use 3 tablespoons
instead of 4 tablespoons.

Stir-Fried Greens

This is an easy recipe to make as a quick accompaniment to a main course.
The water chestnuts give a delicious crunch to the greens.

Serves 4
1 tbsp sunflower oil
1 garlic clove, halved
2 spring onions, sliced finely
200 g/7 oz can water chestnuts, drained and sliced finely
500 g/1 lb 2 oz spinach, tough stalks removed
1 tsp sherry vinegar
1 tsp light soy sauce
pepper

1 Heat the oil in a preheated wok or large, heavy frying pan over a high heat.

2 Add the garlic and cook, stirring, for 1 minute. Be careful not to let the garlic burn on the bottom of the wok or pan.

3 Add the spring onions and water chestnuts, if using, and stir for 2–3 minutes.

4 Stir in the spinach. Add the sherry vinegar, soy sauce and a sprinkling of pepper and cook, stirring, until the spinach is tender. Remove the garlic.

5 Transfer the stir-fried greens to a warmed serving dish, using a slotted spoon in order to drain off the excess liquid. Serve immediately.

Sweet & Sour Vegetables & Tofu

This dish is ideal served with plain noodles for a filling, Oriental meal.

Serves 4
1 tbsp peanut oil
2 garlic cloves, crushed
1 tsp grated root ginger
50 g/1³/₄ oz baby corn cobs
50 g/1³/₄ oz mangetout
1 carrot, cut into matchsticks
1 green pepper, cut into matchsticks
8 spring onions, trimmed
50 g/1³/₄ oz canned bamboo shoots
225 g/8 oz marinated firm tofu, cubed
2 tbsp dry sherry
2 tbsp rice vinegar
2 tbsp clear honey
1 tbsp light soy sauce
150 ml/¹/₄ pint vegetable stock
1 tbsp cornflour

1 Heat the oil in a preheated wok until almost smoking. Add the garlic and ginger and cook for 30 seconds.

2 Add the corn cobs, mangetout, carrot and pepper and stir-fry for 5 minutes or until the vegetables are tender.

3 Add the spring onions, bamboo shoots and tofu and cook for a further 2 minutes.

4 Stir in the sherry, rice vinegar, honey, soy sauce, vegetable stock and cornflour and bring to the boil. Reduce the heat and simmer for 2 minutes. Transfer to serving dishes and serve.

Stir-Fried Winter Vegetables with Coriander

Ordinary winter vegetables are given extraordinary treatment in this
lively stir-fry, just the thing for perking up jaded palates.

Serves 4

3 tbsp sesame oil

25 g/1 oz blanched almonds

1 large carrot, cut into thin strips

1 large turnip, cut into thin strips

1 onion, sliced finely

1 garlic clove, crushed

3 celery sticks, sliced finely

125 g/4^1/$_2$ oz Brussels sprouts,
trimmed and halved

125 g/4^1/$_2$ oz cauliflower,
broken into florets

125 g/4^1/$_2$ oz white cabbage, shredded

2 tsp sesame seeds

1 tsp grated fresh root ginger

^{1}/$_2$ tsp medium chilli powder

1 tbsp chopped fresh coriander

1 tbsp light soy sauce

salt and pepper

sprigs of fresh coriander,
to garnish

4 Add the chopped coriander, soy
sauce, seasoning and almonds to the
mixture, stirring gently. Serve the
vegetables, garnished with a few of
sprigs of fresh coriander.

1 Heat the sesame oil in a preheated
wok or large frying pan. Add the
almonds and stir-fry until lightly
browned. Remove the almonds with
a slotted spoon and drain well on
paper towels.

2 Add all the vegetables to the wok
or frying pan, except for
the cabbage. Stir-fry briskly for
3–4 minutes.

3 Add the cabbage, sesame seeds,
ginger and chilli powder to the
vegetables and cook, stirring, for
2 minutes.

Green Curry with Tempeh

Green curry paste will keep for up to 3 weeks in the refrigerator. If you don't have time to make the green curry paste, it can be bought ready-made (use 6 tablespoons for this recipe).

Serves 4

1 tbsp sunflower oil

175 g/6 oz marinated or plain tempeh, cut into diamonds

6 spring onions, cut into 2.5 cm/1 inch pieces

150 ml/¼ pint coconut milk

grated rind of 1 lime

15 g/½ oz fresh basil leaves

¼ tsp liquid seasoning, such as Maggi

GREEN CURRY PASTE

2 tsp coriander seeds

1 tsp cumin seeds

1 tsp black peppercorns

4 large green chillies, deseeded

2 shallots, quartered

2 garlic cloves, peeled

2 tbsp chopped fresh coriander, including root and stalk

grated rind of 1 lime

1 tbsp roughly chopped galangal

1 tsp ground turmeric

salt

2 tbsp oil

TO GARNISH

fresh coriander leaves

2 green chillies, sliced thinly

1 To make the curry paste, grind the coriander, cumin seeds and the peppercorns in a food processor or pestle and mortar. Blend the remaining ingredients together and add to the ground spice mixture.

2 Heat the oil in a wok or frying pan. Add the tempeh and stir-fry over a high heat for about 2 minutes or until

sealed on all sides. Add the spring onions and stir-fry for 1 minute. Remove the tempeh and spring onions and reserve.

3 Put half of the coconut milk into the wok or pan and bring to the boil. Add 6 tbsp of the curry paste and the lime

rind, and cook for 1 minute. Add the reserved tempeh and spring onions. Add the remaining coconut milk and simmer for 7–8 minutes. Stir in the basil leaves and liquid seasoning and simmer for 1 minute. Garnish with coriander and chillies and serve.

Indonesian Chestnut & Vegetable Stir-Fry with Peanut Sauce

This colourful, spicy stir-fry has an Indonesian influence,
with the shallots, chillies, ginger, fresh coriander and limes.

Serves 4
PEANUT SAUCE
125 g/4¹/₂ oz unsalted roasted peanuts
2 tsp hot chilli sauce
180 ml/6 fl oz coconut milk
2 tbsp soy sauce
1 tbsp ground coriander
pinch of ground turmeric
1 tbsp dark muscovado sugar
STIR-FRY
3 tbsp sesame oil
3–4 shallots, finely sliced
1 garlic clove, finely sliced
1–2 red chillies, deseeded and finely chopped
1 large carrot, cut into fine strips
1 yellow and 1 red pepper, sliced
1 courgette, cut into fine strips
125 g/4¹/₂ oz sugar-snap peas, trimmed
7.5 cm/3 inch piece of cucumber, cut into strips
250 g/9 oz oyster mushrooms,
250 g/9 oz canned chestnuts, drained
2 tsp grated ginger root
finely grated rind and juice of 1 lime
1 tbsp chopped fresh coriander
salt and pepper
lime wedges, to garnish

1 To make the sauce, grind the peanuts in a blender, or chop very finely. Put into a small pan with the remaining ingredients. Heat gently and simmer for 3–4 minutes.

2 Heat the oil in a wok or frying pan. Add the shallots, garlic and chillies and stir-fry for 2 minutes.

3 Add the carrot, peppers, courgette and sugar-snap peas to the wok or pan and stir-fry for 2 minutes.

4 Add the cucumber, mushrooms, chestnuts, ginger, lime rind and juice, coriander and seasoning to the wok or pan and stir-fry briskly for about 5

minutes, or until the vegetables are crisp, yet crunchy.

5 Divide the stir-fry between 4 warmed serving plates, and garnish with lime wedges. Serve with the peanut sauce.

Cauliflower with Oriental Greens

This is a delicious way to cook cauliflower – even without the greens.

Serves 4
175 g/6 oz cauliflower, cut into florets
1 garlic clove
$\frac{1}{2}$ tsp turmeric
1 tbsp coriander root or stem
1 tbsp sunflower oil
2 spring onions, cut into 2.5 cm/1 inch pieces
125 g/4$\frac{1}{2}$ oz oriental greens, such as Thai spinach, bok choy or mustard greens, tough stalks removed
1 tsp yellow mustard seeds

1 Blanch the cauliflower, rinse in cold running water and drain thoroughly. Set aside until required.

2 Grind the garlic, turmeric and coriander root or stem together in a pestle and mortar or spice grinder.

3 Heat the oil in a wok or large, heavy frying pan. Add the spring onions and stir-fry over a high heat for 2 minutes. Add the greens and stir-fry for 1 minute. Remove and set aside.

4 Return the wok or frying pan to the heat. Add the mustard seeds and stir-fry until they start to pop. Add the turmeric mixture and the cauliflower and stir-fry until the cauliflower is coated.

5 Transfer to a warmed serving plate and serve with the greens.

Kidney Bean Kiev

This is a vegetarian version of chicken kiev, the bean patties taking the place of the chicken. Topped with garlic and herb butter and coated in breadcrumbs, this version is just as delicious.

Serves 4
GARLIC BUTTER
100 g/3$^{1}/_2$ oz butter
3 garlic cloves, crushed
1 tbsp chopped parsley
BEAN PATTIES
650 g/1 lb 7 oz canned red kidney beans
150 g/5$^{1}/_2$ oz fresh white breadcrumbs
25 g/1 oz butter
1 leek, chopped
1 celery stick, chopped
1 tbsp chopped parsley
1 egg, beaten
salt and pepper
vegetable oil, for shallow frying

1 To make the garlic butter, put the butter, garlic and parsley in a bowl and blend together with a wooden spoon. Place the garlic butter mixture on to a sheet of greaseproof paper, roll into a cigar shape and wrap in the greaseproof paper. Leave to chill in the refrigerator.

2 Using a potato masher, mash the beans in a mixing bowl and stir in 75 g/2$^3/_4$ oz of the breadcrumbs.

3 Melt the butter in a frying pan and sauté the leek and celery for 3–4 minutes, stirring.

4 Add the bean mixture to the pan together with the parsley, season with salt and pepper to taste and mix well. Remove from the heat and leave to cool slightly.

5 Shape the bean mixture into 4 equal sized ovals.

6 Slice the garlic butter into 4 and place a slice in the centre of each bean patty. Mould the bean mixture around the garlic butter to encase it completely.

7 Dip each bean patty into the beaten egg to coat and then roll in the remaining breadcrumbs.

8 Heat a little oil in a frying pan and fry the patties, turning once, for 7–10 minutes or until golden. Serve.

Vegetable Chop Suey

A classic Chinese dish found on all take-away menus,
this recipe is quick to prepare and makes a tasty meal.

Serves 4
2 tbsp peanut oil
1 onion, chopped
3 garlic cloves, chopped
1 green pepper, diced
1 red pepper, diced
75 g/2³/₄ oz broccoli florets
1 courgette, sliced
25 g/1 oz French beans
1 carrot, cut into matchsticks
100 g/3¹/₂ oz bean-sprouts
2 tsp light brown sugar
2 tbsp light soy sauce
125 ml/4 fl oz vegetable stock
salt and pepper

1 Heat the oil in a preheated wok until almost smoking. Add the onion and garlic and stir-fry for 30 seconds.

2 Stir in the peppers, broccoli, courgette, beans and carrot and stir-fry for a further 2–3 minutes.

3 Add the bean-sprouts, sugar, soy sauce, vegetable stock and salt and pepper to taste and cook for about 2 minutes.

4 Transfer to serving plates and serve immediately with noodles.

COOK'S TIP

Ensure that the vegetable pieces are of the same size in order that they all cook in the stated time.

Vegetable & Feta Cheese Patties

Grated carrots, courgettes and Feta cheese are combined with
cumin seeds, poppy seeds, curry powder and chopped fresh parsley.

Serves 4
2 large carrots
1 large courgette
1 small onion
60 g/2 oz Feta cheese
25 g/1 oz plain flour
1/4 tsp cumin seeds
1/2 tsp poppy seeds
1 tsp medium curry powder
1 tbsp chopped fresh parsley
1 egg, beaten
25 g/1 oz butter
2 tbsp vegetable oil
salt and pepper
sprigs of fresh herbs, to garnish

1 Grate the carrots, courgette, onion and Feta cheese coarsely, either by hand or in a food processor.

2 Mix together the flour, cumin seeds, poppy seeds, curry powder and parsley in a large bowl. Season well with salt and pepper.

3 Add the vegetable and Feta cheese mixture to the seasoned flour, tossing well to combine. Stir in the beaten egg and mix well.

4 Heat the butter and oil in a large frying pan. Place heaped tablespoonfuls of the vegetable and cheese mixture in the pan, flattening them slightly with the back of the spoon. Fry gently for about 2 minutes on each side, until crisp and golden brown. Drain the patties on paper towels and keep warm until they have all been cooked.

5 Garnish with sprigs of fresh herbs and serve.

COOK'S VARIATION

Omit the cumin and curry powder; use 1 tbsp oregano for the parsley.

Golden Cheese, Leek & Potato Cakes

Make these tasty potato cakes for a quick and simple supper dish.
Serve them with scrambled eggs if you're very hungry.

Serves 4
1 kg/2 lb 4 oz potatoes
4 tbsp milk
60 g/2 oz butter
or vegetarian margarine
2 leeks, chopped finely
1 onion, chopped finely
175 g/6 oz grated mature
Cheddar
1 tbsp chopped fresh parsley
or chives
1 egg, beaten
2 tbsp water
90 g/3 oz fresh white
or brown breadcrumbs
vegetable oil, for shallow frying
salt and pepper
fresh flat-leaf parsley sprigs,
to garnish
tomato salad and cucumber and
sweetcorn relish, to serve

1 Cook the potatoes in a saucepan of lightly salted boiling water until tender. Drain thoroughly. Mash the potatoes with the milk and the butter or margarine.

2 Cook the leeks and onion in a small amount of salted boiling water for about 10 minutes until tender. Drain.

3 In a large mixing bowl, combine the leeks and onion with the mashed potato, cheese and parsley or chives. Season to taste.

4 Beat the egg and water together in a bowl. Sprinkle the breadcrumbs into a separate bowl.

5 Shape the potato mixture into 12 cakes. Brush each cake with the egg mixture, then coat in the breadcrumbs.

6 Heat the oil in a large frying pan and fry the potato cakes gently, in batches, for 2–3 minutes on each side or until light golden brown. Garnish with flat-leaf parsley and serve with a tomato salad and relish.

Sauté of Summer Vegetables with Tarragon Dressing

The freshness of lightly cooked summer vegetables is enhanced by the aromatic flavour of a tarragon and white wine dressing.

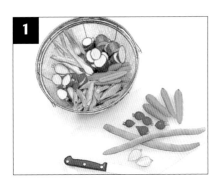

Serves 4
250 g/9 oz baby carrots, scrubbed
125 g/4¹/₂ oz runner beans
2 courgettes, trimmed
1 bunch large spring onions, trimmed
1 bunch radishes, trimmed
60 g/2 oz butter
2 tbsp light olive oil
2 tbsp white wine vinegar
4 tbsp dry white wine
1 tsp caster sugar
1 tbsp chopped fresh tarragon
salt and pepper
sprigs of fresh tarragon, to garnish

1 Trim and halve the carrots, slice the beans and courgettes, and halve the spring onions and radishes, so that all of the vegetables are cut to even-sized pieces.

2 Melt the butter in a large frying pan or wok. Add all of the vegetables and stir-fry over a medium heat, stirring frequently.

3 Heat the olive oil, vinegar, white wine, sugar and salt and pepper to taste in a small saucepan. Remove from the heat and add the tarragon.

4 When the vegetables are just cooked, but still retain their crunchiness, pour over the 'dressing'. Stir through, and then transfer to a warmed serving dish. Garnish with sprigs of fresh tarragon and serve at once.

Sweetcorn Patties

These are a delicious addition to any party buffet, and are very simple to prepare.
Serve with a sweet chilli sauce.

Makes 12
325 g/11½ oz can sweetcorn, drained
1 onion, chopped finely
1 tsp curry powder
1 garlic clove, crushed
1 tsp ground coriander
2 spring onions, chopped
3 tbsp plain flour
½ tsp baking powder
salt
1 large egg
4 tbsp sunflower oil
spring onions, sliced diagonally, to garnish

1 Mash the drained sweetcorn lightly in a medium-sized bowl.

2 Add all the remaining ingredients, except for the oil, one at a time, stirring after each addition.

3 Heat the sunflower oil in a frying pan. Drop tablespoonfuls of the mixture carefully into the hot oil, far enough apart for them not to run into each other as they cook. Alternatively, cook the patties one at a time. Cook the patties for 4–5 minutes, turning each patty once, until golden brown and firm. Take care not to turn them too soon, or they will break up in the pan.

4 Remove the patties from the pan and drain on paper towels. Serve quickly while still warm.

Bakes & Roasts

Anyone who ever thought that vegetarian meals were dull will be proved very wrong by the rich variety of dishes in this chapter. You'll recognize influences from all over the world, but there are also traditional stews and casseroles as well as hearty bakes and roasts. They all make exciting eating at any time of year, and for virtually any occasion. There are lots of ideas for mid-week meals

or for entertaining, some traditional and some more unusual.

Some of the ingredients may be unfamiliar but you should have no difficulty in buying them from health food stores or large supermarkets. Don't be afraid to substitute ingredients where appropriate. There is no reason why you cannot enjoy experimenting and adding your own touch to these imaginative ideas.

Chick-pea Roast with Sherry Sauce

This is a vegetarian version of the classic 'Beef Wellington', and just as delicious.
Served with a sherry sauce and roast vegetables it makes a tasty and impressive main dish.

Serves 4
450 g/1 lb can chick-peas, drained
1 tsp marmite
150 g/5^1/$_2$ oz chopped walnuts
150 g/5^1/$_2$ oz fresh white breadcrumbs
1 onion, finely chopped
100 g/3^1/$_2$ oz mushrooms, sliced
50 g/1^3/$_4$ oz canned sweetcorn, drained
2 garlic cloves, crushed
2 tbsp dry sherry
2 tbsp vegetable stock
1 tbsp chopped coriander
225 g/8 oz prepared puff pastry
1 egg, beaten
2 tbsp milk
salt and pepper

SAUCE

1 tbsp vegetable oil
1 leek, thinly sliced
4 tbsp dry sherry
150 ml/^{1}/$_4$ pint vegetable stock

1 Put the chick-peas, marmite, nuts, and breadcrumbs in a food processor and blend for 30 seconds. Put the onion and mushrooms in a large frying pan and sauté in their own juices for 3–4 minutes.

2 Stir the chick-pea mixture into the pan with the sweetcorn and garlic. Stir in the sherry, stock, coriander and seasoning and bind the mixture together. Remove from the heat and allow to cool.

3 Roll the pastry out on to a lightly floured surface to form a 35.5 cm/ 14 inch × 30 cm/12 inch rectangle.

4 Shape the chick-pea mixture into a loaf shape and wrap the pastry around it, sealing the edges. Place seam-side down on a dampened baking sheet and score the top in a criss-cross pattern. Mix the egg and milk and brush over the pastry to glaze. Cook in a preheated oven, 200°C/400°F/Gas Mark 6, for 25–30 minutes or until

risen and golden. Heat the oil for the sauce in a pan and sauté the leek for 5 minutes, stirring. Add the remaining ingredients and bring to the boil. Simmer for 5 minutes and serve with the roast.

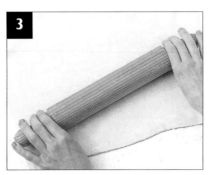

Savoury Bread & Butter Pudding

Quick, simple and nutritious – what more could
you ask for an inexpensive mid-week meal?

 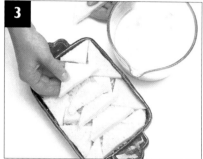 

Serves 4

60 g/2 oz butter or
vegetarian margarine

1 bunch spring onions,
sliced

6 slices white or brown bread,
crusts removed

175g/6 oz grated mature
Cheddar

2 eggs

425 ml/³/₄ pint milk

salt and pepper

sprigs of fresh flat-leaf parsley,
to garnish

1 Grease a 1.5 litre/2³/₄ pint baking
dish with a little of the butter or
margarine. Melt the remaining butter
or margarine in a small saucepan and
fry the spring onions until softened
and golden.

2 Cut the bread into triangles and
layer half of them in the baking dish.
Top with the spring onions and half
of the cheese.

3 Beat together the eggs and milk and
season with salt and pepper to taste.
Layer the remaining triangles of bread
in the dish and carefully pour over
the milk mixture. Leave to soak for
15–20 minutes.

4 Sprinkle the remaining cheese over
the soaked bread. Bake in a preheated
oven, 190°C/375°F/Gas Mark 5, for
35–40 minutes or until puffed up and
golden brown. Garnish with flat-leaf
parsley and serve at once.

Mushroom & Nut Crumble

A filling, tasty dish that is ideal for a warming family supper.
The crunchy topping is flavoured with three different types of nuts.

Serves 4

350 g/12 oz open-cup mushrooms, sliced

350 g/12 oz chestnut mushrooms, sliced

400 ml/14 fl oz Fresh
Vegetable Stock (see page 14)

60 g/2 oz/¼ cup butter or vegetarian
margarine

1 large onion, chopped finely

1 garlic clove, crushed

60 g/2 oz plain flour

4 tbsp double cream

2 tbsp chopped fresh parsley

salt and pepper

fresh herbs, to garnish

CRUMBLE TOPPING

90 g/3 oz medium oatmeal

90 g/3 oz wholemeal
flour

25 g/1 oz ground almonds

25 g/1 oz finely chopped walnuts

60 g/2 oz finely chopped unsalted shelled
pistachio nuts

1 tsp dried thyme

90 g/3 oz butter or vegetarian margarine,
softened

1 tbsp fennel seeds

1 Put the mushrooms and stock in a large saucepan, bring to the boil, cover and simmer for 15 minutes until tender. Drain the mushrooms, reserving the stock.

2 In another saucepan, melt the butter or margarine, and gently fry the onion and garlic for 2–3 minutes until just softened but not browned. Stir in the flour and cook for about 1 minute.

3 Remove the pan from the heat and stir in the reserved stock. Return to the heat and cook, stirring, until thickened. Stir in the mushrooms, seasoning, cream and parsley and spoon into a shallow ovenproof dish.

4 To make the topping, mix together the oatmeal, flour, nuts, thyme and plenty of seasoning.

5 Using a fork, mix in the butter or margarine until the topping resembles coarse breadcrumbs.

6 Sprinkle the mixture over the mushrooms, sprinkle with fennel seeds and bake in a preheated oven, 190°C/375°F/Gas Mark 5, for 25–30 minutes until golden and crisp. Garnish with herbs and serve.

Spicy Potato & Lemon Casserole

This is based on a Moroccan dish in which potatoes are spiced
with coriander and cumin and cooked in a lemon sauce.

Serves 4
100 ml/3¹/₂ fl oz olive oil
2 red onions, cut into eight
3 garlic cloves, crushed
2 tsp ground cumin
2 tsp ground coriander
pinch of cayenne pepper
1 carrot, thickly sliced
2 small turnips, quartered
1 courgette, sliced
450 g/1 lb potatoes, thickly sliced
juice and rind of 2 large lemons
300 ml/¹/₂ pint vegetable stock
2 tbsp chopped coriander
salt and pepper

1 Heat the olive oil in a flameproof casserole.

2 Add the red onion and sauté for 3 minutes, stirring.

3 Add the garlic and cook for 30 seconds. Mix in the cumin, ground coriander and cayenne pepper and cook for 1 minute, stirring.

4 Add the carrot, turnips, courgette and potatoes and stir to coat in the olive oil.

5 Add the lemon juice and rind, stock and salt and pepper to taste, cover and cook over a medium heat for 20–30 minutes, stirring occasionally.

6 Remove the lid, sprinkle in the coriander and stir well. Serve immediately.

COOK'S TIP

A selection of spices and herbs is important for adding variety to your cooking – add to your range each time you try a new recipe.

COOK'S TIP

Check the vegetables whilst cooking as they may begin to stick to the pan. Add a little more boiling water or stock if necessary.

Lentil Roast

The perfect dish to serve for an alternative Sunday lunch.
Roasted vegetables make a succulent accompaniment.

Serves 6
250 g/9 oz red lentils
500 ml/18 fl oz Fresh Vegetable Stock (see page 14)
1 bay leaf
15 g/^{1}/$_2$ oz butter or vegetarian margarine, softened
2 tbsp dried wholemeal breadcrumbs
250 g/9 oz grated mature Cheddar
1 leek, chopped finely
125 g/4^1/$_2$ oz button mushrooms, chopped finely
90 g/3 oz fresh wholemeal breadcrumbs
2 tbsp chopped fresh parsley
1 tbsp lemon juice
2 eggs, beaten lightly
salt and pepper
sprigs of fresh flat-leaf parsley, to garnish
mixed roasted vegetables, to serve

1 Put the lentils, stock and bay leaf in a saucepan. Bring to the boil, cover and simmer gently for 15–20 minutes or until all of the liquid is absorbed and the lentils have softened. Discard the bay leaf.

2 Line the base of a 1 kg/2 lb 4 oz loaf tin with baking parchment. Grease the tin with the butter or margarine and sprinkle with the dried breadcrumbs.

3 Stir the cheese, leek, mushrooms, fresh breadcrumbs and parsley into the lentils and season to taste. Bind the mixture together with the lemon juice and eggs.

4 Spoon the mixture into the prepared loaf tin and smooth the top. Bake in a preheated oven, 190°C/375°F/Gas Mark 5, for 1 hour until golden. Loosen the loaf with a palette knife and turn out on to a warmed serving plate. Garnish with parsley and serve sliced with a selection of roasted vegetables.

Winter Vegetable Cobbler

Seasonal fresh vegetables are casseroled with lentils then topped with
a ring of fresh cheese scones to make this tasty cobbler.

Serves 4

1 tbsp olive oil
1 garlic clove, crushed
8 small onions, halved
2 celery stalks, sliced
250 g/9 oz swede, chopped
2 carrots, sliced
1/2 small cauliflower, broken into florets
250 g/9 oz mushrooms, sliced
400 g/14 oz can chopped tomatoes
60 g/2 oz red lentils
2 tbsp cornflour
3–4 tbsp water
300 ml/1/2 pint Fresh Vegetable Stock (see page 14)
2 tsp Tabasco sauce
2 tsp chopped fresh oregano or parsley
sprigs of oregano, to garnish

COBBLER TOPPING

250 g/9 oz self-raising flour
60 g/2 oz butter
125 g/41/2 oz grated Cheddar
2 tsp chopped fresh oregano or parsley
1 egg, beaten
150 ml/1/4 pint skimmed milk
salt

1 Heat the oil in a large pan and fry the garlic and onions for 5 minutes. Add the celery, swede, carrots and cauliflower and fry for 2–3 minutes.

2 Remove the pan from the heat and add the mushrooms, tomatoes and lentils. Mix the cornflour with the water and add to the pan with the stock, Tabasco sauce and oregano or parsley. Bring to the boil, stirring, until thickened. Transfer to an ovenproof dish, cover and bake in a preheated oven, 180°C/350°F/Gas Mark 4, for 20 minutes.

3 To make the topping, sift the flour and salt into a bowl. Rub in the butter, then stir in most of the cheese and the herbs. Beat the egg and milk and add enough to the dry ingredients to make a dough. Knead and roll out to 1 cm/1/2 inch thick. Cut into 5 cm/2 inch rounds. Remove the dish from the oven and increase the temperature to 200°C/400°F/Gas Mark 6. Arrange the rounds around the edge of the dish, brush with the egg and milk and sprinkle with the cheese. Cook for 10–12 minutes. Garnish and serve.

Roast Pepper Tart

This tastes truly delicious, the flavour of roasted vegetables being entirely different from that of boiled or fried.

Serves 8
PASTRY
175 g/6 oz plain flour
pinch of salt
75 g/2¾ oz butter or vegetarian margarine
2 tbsp green pitted olives, finely chopped
3 tbsp cold water
FILLING
1 red pepper
1 green pepper
1 yellow pepper
2 garlic cloves, crushed
2 tbsp olive oil
100 g/3½ oz Mozzarella cheese, grated
2 eggs beaten
150 ml/5 fl oz milk
1 tbsp chopped basil
salt and pepper

1 To make the pastry, sieve the flour and a pinch of salt into a mixing bowl. Rub in the butter or margarine until the mixture resembles breadcrumbs. Add the olives and cold water, bringing the mixture together to form a dough.

2 Roll the dough out on to a floured surface and use to line a 20 cm/8 inch loose-bottomed flan tin. Prick the base with a fork and leave to chill.

3 Cut the peppers in half lengthwise and lay skin-side uppermost on a baking sheet. Mix the garlic and oil and brush over the peppers. Cook in a preheated oven, 200°C/400°F/ Gas Mark 6, for 20 minutes or until beginning to char slightly. Let cool slightly and thinly slice. Arrange in the base of the pastry case, layering with the Mozzarella cheese. Beat the egg and milk and add the basil. Season and pour over the peppers. Put the tart on a baking sheet and return to the oven for 20–25 minutes or until set. Serve hot or cold.

COOK'S TIP

Make sure that the olives are very finely chopped, otherwise they will make holes in the pastry. They should be almost paste-like in consistency and could be chopped in a food processor for ease and speed.

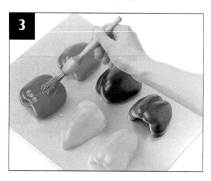

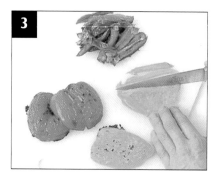

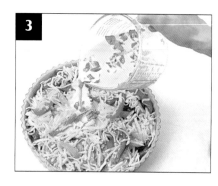

Creamy Baked Fennel

Fennel tastes fabulous in this creamy sauce, flavoured with caraway seeds.
A crunchy breadcrumb topping gives an interesting change of texture.

Serves 4
2 tbsp lemon juice
2 fennel bulbs, trimmed
125 g/4$\frac{1}{2}$ oz low-fat soft cheese
150 ml/$\frac{1}{4}$ pint single cream
150 ml/$\frac{1}{4}$ pint milk
1 egg, beaten
60 g/2 oz butter
2 tsp caraway seeds
60 g/2 oz fresh white breadcrumbs
salt and pepper
sprigs of flat-leaf parsley, to garnish

1 Bring a large saucepan of water to the boil and add the lemon juice. Slice the bulbs of fennel thinly and add them to the saucepan. Cook for 2–3 minutes to blanch, and then drain.

2 Arrange the slices of fennel in a buttered ovenproof baking dish.

3 Beat the soft cheese in a bowl until smooth. Add the cream, milk and beaten egg and whisk together until combined. Season with salt and pepper to taste and pour the mixture over the fennel.

4 Melt 15 g/$\frac{1}{2}$ oz of the butter in a small frying pan and fry the caraway seeds gently for 1–2 minutes, to release their flavour and aroma. Sprinkle them over the fennel.

5 Melt the remaining butter in a frying pan.

6 Add the breadcrumbs to the frying pan and fry gently until lightly browned. Sprinkle the breadcrumbs evenly over the surface of the fennel.

7 Cook in a preheated oven, 180°C/350°F/Gas Mark 4, for 25–30 minutes, or until the fennel is tender. Transfer to serving plates, garnish with sprigs of parsley and serve.

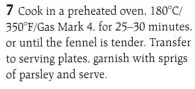

Mexican Chilli Corn Pie

This bake of sweetcorn and kidney beans, flavoured with chilli and fresh coriander, is topped with crispy cheese cornbread.

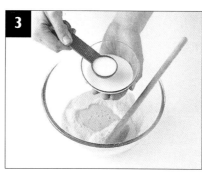

Serves 4
1 tbsp corn oil
2 garlic cloves, crushed
1 red pepper, deseeded and diced
1 green pepper, deseeded and diced
1 celery stalk, diced
1 tsp hot chilli powder
400 g/14 oz can chopped tomatoes
325 g/11$^{1}/_{2}$ oz can sweetcorn, drained
215 g/7$^{1}/_{2}$ oz can kidney beans, drained and rinsed
2 tbsp chopped fresh coriander
salt and pepper
sprigs of fresh coriander, to garnish
tomato and avocado salad, to serve

TOPPING
125 g/4$^{1}/_{2}$ oz cornmeal
1 tbsp plain flour
$^{1}/_{2}$ tsp salt
2 tsp baking powder
1 egg, beaten
100 ml/3$^{1}/_{2}$ fl oz milk
1 tbsp corn oil
125 g/4$^{1}/_{2}$ oz grated mature Cheddar

1 Heat the oil in a large frying pan and gently fry the garlic, peppers and celery for 5–6 minutes or until just softened.

2 Stir in the chilli powder, tomatoes, sweetcorn, beans and seasoning. Bring to the boil and simmer for 10 minutes. Stir in the coriander and spoon into an ovenproof dish.

3 To make the topping, mix together the cornmeal, flour, salt and baking powder. Make a well in the centre, add the egg, milk and oil and beat until a smooth batter is formed.

4 Spoon over the pepper and sweetcorn mixture and sprinkle with the cheese. Bake in a preheated oven, 220°C/425°F/Gas Mark 7, for 25–30 minutes until golden and firm.

5 Garnish with fresh coriander sprigs and serve immediately with a tomato and avocado salad.

Cauliflower, Broccoli & Cheese Flan

This really is a tasty flan, the pastry case for which may
be made in advance and frozen until required.

Serves 8
PASTRY
175 g/6 oz plain flour
pinch of salt
1/2 tsp paprika
1 tsp dried thyme
75 g/2³/4 oz/6 tbsp vegetarian margarine
3 tbsp water
FILLING
100 g/3¹/2 oz cauliflower florets
100 g/3¹/2 oz broccoli florets
1 onion, cut into eight
2 tbsp butter or vegetarian margarine
1 tbsp plain flour
85 ml/3 fl oz vegetable stock
125 ml/4 fl oz milk
75 g/2³/4 oz vegetarian Cheddar cheese, grated
salt and pepper
paprika and thyme, to garnish

1 To make the pastry, sieve the flour and salt into a bowl. Add the paprika and thyme and rub the margarine into the mixture until it resembles breadcrumbs. Stir in the water and bring together to form a dough.

2 Roll the pastry out on a floured surface and use to line an 18cm/7 inch loose-bottomed flan tin. Prick the base with a fork and line with baking parchment. Fill with ceramic baking beans and bake blind in a preheated oven, at 190°C/375°F/Gas Mark 5, for 15 minutes. Remove the parchment and beans and return the pastry case to the oven for 5 minutes.

3 To make the filling, cook the cauliflower, broccoli and onion in a pan of boiling water for 10–12 minutes until tender. Drain and reserve.

4 Melt the butter in a pan. Add the flour and cook, stirring, for 1 minute. Remove from the heat, stir in the stock and milk and return to the heat.

Bring to the boil, stirring, and add 50g/1³/4 oz of the cheese. Season.

5 Spoon the cauliflower, broccoli and onion into the pastry case. Pour over the sauce and sprinkle with the cheese. Return to the oven for 10 minutes until the cheese is bubbling. Dust with paprika and garnish with thyme. Serve.

Vegetable Jalousie

This is a really easy dish to make, but looks impressive.
The mixture of vegetables gives the dish a wonderful colour and flavour.

Serves 4
450 g/1 lb prepared puff pastry
1 egg, beaten
FILLING
2 tbsp butter or vegetarian margarine
1 leek, shredded
2 garlic cloves, crushed
1 red pepper, sliced
1 yellow pepper, sliced
50 g/1¾ oz mushrooms, sliced
75 g/2¾ oz small asparagus spears
2 tbsp flour
85 ml/3 fl oz vegetable stock
85 ml/3 fl oz milk
4 tbsp dry white wine
1 tbsp chopped oregano
salt and pepper

1 Melt the butter or margarine in a saucepan and sauté the leek and garlic for 2 minutes, stirring. Add the remaining vegetables and cook, stirring for 3–4 minutes.

2 Add the flour and cook for 1 minute. Remove the pan from the heat and stir in the stock, milk and wine. Return the pan to the heat and bring to the boil, stirring, until thickened. Stir in the oregano and season with salt and pepper to taste.

3 Roll half of the pastry out on a lightly floured surface to form a rectangle 42.5 cm/15 inches × 15 cm/6 inches. Roll out the other half of the pastry to the same shape, but a little larger. Put the smaller rectangle on a baking sheet (cookie sheet) lined with dampened baking parchment.

4 Spoon the filling on top of the smaller rectangle, leaving a 1.25 cm/½ inch clean edge.

5 Cut parallel slits across the larger rectangle to within 2.5 cm/1 inch of each edge.

6 Brush the edge of the smaller rectangle with egg and place the larger rectangle on top, sealing the edges well.

7 Brush the whole jalousie with egg and cook in a preheated oven, 200°C/400°F/Gas Mark 6, for 30–35 minutes until risen and golden. Serve immediately.

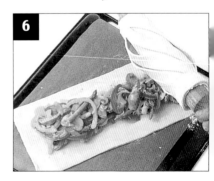

Spanish Pancake Layer

Nutty-tasting buckwheat pancakes are combined with a cheesy spinach
mixture and baked with a crispy topping.

Serves 4
125 g/4^1/$_2$ oz buckwheat flour
1 egg, beaten
1 tbsp walnut oil
300 ml/^{1}/$_2$ pint milk
2 tsp vegetable oil

FILLING
1 kg/2 lb 4 oz young spinach leaves
2 tbsp water
1 bunch spring onions, white and green parts, chopped
2 tsp walnut oil
1 egg, beaten
1 egg yolk
250 g/9 oz cottage cheese
^{1}/$_2$ tsp grated nutmeg
25 g/1 oz grated Cheddar cheese
25 g/1 oz walnut pieces
salt and pepper

1 Sift the flour into a bowl and add any husks that remain behind in the sieve. Make a well in the centre and add the egg and walnut oil. Whisk in the milk to make a smooth batter. Leave to stand for 30 minutes.

2 To make the filling, wash the spinach and pack into a pan with the water. Cover tightly and cook on a high heat for 5–6 minutes until soft. Drain well and leave to cool. Fry the spring onions in the walnut oil for 2–3 minutes until just soft. Drain and set aside.

3 Whisk the batter. Brush a crêpe pan with vegetable oil, heat until hot and pour in enough batter to lightly cover the base. Cook for 1–2 minutes until set, turn and cook for 1 minute until golden. Repeat to make 8–10 pancakes, layering them with parchment. Chop the spinach and pat dry with paper towels. Mix with the spring onions, beaten egg, egg yolk, cottage cheese, nutmeg and seasoning.

4 Layer the spinach mixture between the pancakes on a baking sheet lined with baking parchment, finishing with a pancake. Sprinkle with Cheddar. Bake in a preheated oven, 190°C/375°F/Gas Mark 5, for 20–25 minutes until firm and golden. Sprinkle with the walnuts and serve.

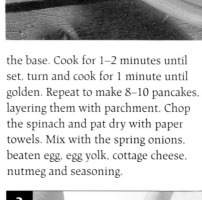

Cauliflower Bake

The red of the tomatoes is a great contrast to the cauliflower and herbs,
making this dish appealing to both the eye and the palate.

Serves 4
450 g/1 lb cauliflower
2 large potatoes, cubed
100 g/3$^{1}/_{2}$ oz cherry tomatoes

SAUCE

25 g/1 oz butter or vegetarian margarine
1 leek, sliced
1 garlic clove, crushed
25 g/1 oz plain flour
300 ml/$^{1}/_{2}$ pint milk
75 g/2$^{3}/_{4}$ oz mixed grated cheese, such as Cheddar, Parmesan and Gruyère
$^{1}/_{2}$ tsp paprika
2 tbsp chopped flat-leaf parsley
salt and pepper

1 Cook the cauliflower in a saucepan of boiling water for 10 minutes. Drain well and reserve. Meanwhile, cook the potatoes in a pan of boiling water for 10 minutes, drain and reserve.

2 To make the sauce, melt the butter or margarine in a pan and sauté the leek and garlic for 1 minute. Add the flour and cook for 1 minute. Remove the pan from the heat and gradually stir in the milk, 50 g/1$^{3}/_{4}$ oz of the cheese, the paprika and parsley. Return the pan to the heat and bring to the boil, stirring. Season.

3 Spoon the cauliflower into a deep ovenproof dish. Add the cherry tomatoes and top with the potatoes to cover. Pour the sauce over the top of the potatoes and sprinkle on the remaining cheese.

4 Cook in a preheated oven, 180°C/350°F/Gas Mark 4, for 20 minutes or until the vegetables are cooked through and the cheese is golden brown and bubbling. Serve immediately.

COOK'S VARIATION

This dish could be made with broccoli instead of the cauliflower as an alternative.

Root Croustades with Sunshine Peppers

This colourful combination of grated root vegetables and mixed peppers would make a stunning dinner-party dish.

Serves 4

1 orange pepper
1 red pepper
1 yellow pepper
3 tbsp olive oil
2 tbsp red wine vinegar
1 tsp French mustard
1 tsp clear honey
salt and pepper
sprigs of fresh flat-leaf parsley, to garnish
green vegetables, to serve

CROUSTADES

250 g/9 oz potatoes, grated
250 g/9 oz carrots, grated
350 g/12 oz celeriac, grated
1 garlic clove, crushed
1 tbsp lemon juice
25 g/1 oz butter or
vegetarian margarine, melted
1 egg, beaten
1 tbsp vegetable oil

3 To make the croustades, mix the potatoes, carrots and celeriac; toss in the garlic and lemon juice. Mix in the butter or margarine and the egg. Season. Divide the mixture into 8 and pile on to 2 baking sheets lined with baking parchment, forming each into a

10 cm/ 4 inch round. Brush with oil. Bake in a preheated oven, 220°C/ 425°F/Gas Mark 7, for 30–35 minutes until crisp and golden. Heat the peppers and the marinade for 2–3 minutes, then spoon over the croustades, garnish and serve.

1 Place the peppers on a baking sheet. Bake in a preheated oven, 190°C/375°F/Gas Mark 5, for 35 minutes, turning after 20 minutes. Remove the peppers from the oven, cover with a tea towel and let cool for 10 minutes. Peel the skin from the cooked peppers; cut in half and discard the seeds. Thinly slice the flesh into strips and place in a shallow dish.

2 Put the oil, vinegar, mustard, honey and seasoning in a screw-top jar and shake to mix. Pour over the pepper strips, toss to mix and leave to marinate for 2 hours.

Spicy Stuffed Chinese Leaves

Mushrooms, spring onions, celery and rice are flavoured
with five-spice powder and wrapped in Chinese leaves.

Serves 4
8 large Chinese leaves
60 g/2 oz long-grain rice
$^1/_2$ vegetable stock cube
60 g/2 oz butter
1 bunch spring onions, trimmed and chopped finely
1 celery stalk, chopped finely
125 g/4$^1/_2$ oz button mushrooms, sliced
1 tsp Chinese five-spice powder
300 ml/$^1/_2$ pint passata
salt and pepper
fresh chives, to garnish

1 Blanch the Chinese leaves in a saucepan of boiling water for about 1 minute. Refresh under cold running water and drain well. Be careful not to tear the leaves.

2 Cook the rice in a saucepan of boiling water, with the stock cube, for 15–20 minutes or until just tender. Drain well.

3 Meanwhile, melt the butter in a frying pan and fry the spring onions and celery gently for 3–4 minutes until softened, but not browned. Add the mushrooms and cook for a further 3–4 minutes, stirring frequently.

4 Add the cooked rice and Chinese five-spice powder to the frying pan. Season with salt and pepper to taste and stir well to combine the ingredients.

5 Lay out the Chinese leaves on a chopping board and divide the rice mixture between them. Roll each leaf into a neat parcel to enclose the stuffing. Place the Chinese leaves, seam-side down, in a greased ovenproof dish.

6 Pour the passata over them and cover with foil.

7 Bake in a preheated oven, 190°C/ 375°F/Gas Mark 5, for 25–30 minutes. Serve immediately, garnished with fresh chives.

Artichoke & Cheese Flan

Artichoke hearts are delicious to eat, being very delicate in flavour and appearance.
They are ideal for cooking in a cheese-flavoured pastry case.

Serves 8

175 g/6 oz wholemeal flour
2 garlic cloves, crushed
75 g/2³⁄4 oz butter or
vegetarian margarine
salt and pepper

FILLING

2 tbsp olive oil
1 red onion, halved and sliced
10 canned or fresh artichoke hearts
100 g/3¹⁄2 oz vegetarian
Cheddar, grated
50 g/1³⁄4 oz Gorgonzola cheese,
crumbled
2 eggs, beaten
1 tbsp chopped fresh rosemary
150 ml/¹⁄4 pint milk

1 To make the pastry, sieve the flour into a mixing bowl, add a pinch of salt and the garlic. Rub in the butter or margarine until the mixture resembles breadcrumbs. Stir in 3 tablespoons of water and bring the mixture together to form a dough.

2 Roll the pastry out on a lightly floured surface to fit a 20cm/8 inch flan tin. Prick the pastry with a fork.

3 Heat the oil in a frying pan and sauté the onion for 3 minutes. Add the artichoke hearts and cook for a further 2 minutes.

4 Mix the cheeses with the beaten eggs, rosemary and milk. Stir in the drained artichoke mixture and season

with salt and pepper to taste.

5 Spoon the artichoke and cheese mixture into the pastry case and cook in a preheated oven, 200°C/400°F/ Gas Mark 6, for 25 minutes or until cooked and set. Serve the flan hot or cold.

COOK'S TIP

Gently press the centre of the
flan with your fingertip to test
if it is cooked through. It should feel
fairly firm, but not solid. If overcooked
the flan will begin
to 'weep'.

Mushroom & Spinach Puff Pastry Parcels

These puff parcels are easy to make and delicious to eat. Filled with garlic, mushrooms and spinach they are ideal with a fresh tomato or cheese sauce.

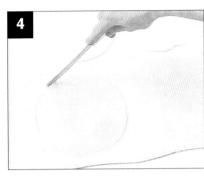

Serves 4
2 tbsp butter
1 red onion, halved and sliced
2 garlic cloves, crushed
225 g/8 oz open-cup mushrooms, sliced
175 g/6 oz baby spinach
pinch of nutmeg
4 tbsp double cream
225 g/8 oz prepared puff pastry
1 egg, beaten
salt and pepper
2 tsp poppy seeds

1 Melt the butter in a frying pan. Add the onion and garlic to the pan and sauté for 3–4 minutes, stirring well.

2 Add the mushrooms, spinach and nutmeg and cook for a further 2–3 minutes.

3 Stir in the cream, mixing well. Season with salt and pepper to taste and remove the pan from the heat.

4 Roll the pastry out on a lightly floured surface and cut into four 15 cm/6 inch circles.

5 Spoon a quarter of the filling on to one half of each circle and fold the pastry over to encase the filling. Seal the edges of the pastry and brush with the beaten egg. Sprinkle with the poppy seeds.

6 Place the parcels on to a dampened baking sheet and cook in a preheated oven, 200°C/400°F/Gas Mark 6, for 20 minutes until risen and golden brown.

7 Transfer the mushroom and spinach puff pastry parcels to serving plates and serve immediately.

COOK'S TIP

The baking sheet is dampened so that steam forms with the heat of the oven and helps the pastry to rise and set.

Vegetable & Tofu Strudels

These strudels look really impressive and are perfect if friends are coming
round or for a more formal dinner party dish.

Serves 4

FILLING

2 tbsp vegetable oil

2 tbsp butter or vegetarian margarine

150 g/5$^{1}/_{2}$ oz potatoes finely diced

1 leek, shredded

2 garlic cloves, crushed

1 tsp garam masala

$^{1}/_{2}$ tsp chilli powder

$^{1}/_{2}$ tsp turmeric

50 g/1$^{3}/_{4}$ oz okra, sliced

100 g/3$^{1}/_{2}$ oz button mushrooms,
sliced

2 tomatoes, diced

225 g/8 oz firm tofu, diced

12 sheets filo pastry

2 tbsp butter or vegetarian margarine,
melted

salt and pepper

1 To make the filling, heat the oil and
butter in a frying pan. Add the
potatoes and leek and cook for 2–3
minutes, stirring.

2 Add the garlic and spices, okra,
mushrooms, tomatoes, tofu and
seasoning and cook, stirring, for 5–7
minutes or until tender.

3 Lay the pastry out on a chopping
board and brush each individual sheet
with butter. Place 3 sheets on top of
one another; repeat to make 4 stacks.

4 Spoon a quarter of the filling along
the centre of each stack and brush the
edges with butter. Fold the short
edges in and roll up lengthwise to
form a cigar shape; brush the outside

with butter. Place the strudels on a
greased baking sheet.

5 Cook in a preheated oven, 190°C/
375°F/Gas Mark 5, and cook the
strudels for 20 minutes or until
golden brown. Serve immediately.

COOK'S TIP

Decorate the outside of the
strudels with crumpled pastry
trimmings before cooking for a really
impressive effect.

Vegetable Toad-in-the-hole

This dish can be made in one large dish or in
individual Yorkshire pudding tins.

Serves 4
BATTER
100 g/3½ oz plain flour
2 eggs, beaten
200 ml/7 fl oz milk
2 tbsp wholegrain mustard
2 tbsp vegetable oil
FILLING
2 tbsp butter
2 garlic cloves, crushed
1 onion, cut into eight
75 g/2¾ oz baby carrots, halved lengthwise
50 g/1¾ oz French beans
50 g/1¾ oz canned sweetcorn, drained
2 tomatoes, seeded and cut into chunks
1 tsp wholegrain mustard
1 tbsp chopped mixed herbs
salt and pepper

1 To make the batter, sieve the flour
and a pinch of salt into a large bowl.
Make a well in the centre and beat in
the eggs and milk to make a batter.
Stir in the mustard and leave to stand.

2 Pour the vegetable oil into a
shallow ovenproof dish and heat in
a preheated oven, 200°C/400°F/Gas
Mark 6, for 10 minutes.

3 Meanwhile, make the filling. Melt
the butter in a frying pan and sauté
the garlic and onion for 2 minutes,
stirring. Cook the carrots and beans in
a saucepan of boiling water for 7
minutes or until tender. Drain well.

4 Add the sweetcorn and tomato
to the frying pan with the mustard
and herbs. Season well and add the
carrots and beans.

5 Remove the dish from the oven
and pour in the batter. Spoon the
vegetables into the centre, return to
the oven and cook for 30–35 minutes
until the batter has risen and set.

6 Serve the vegetable toad-in-the-hole
immediately.

COOK'S TIP

It is important that the oil is hot
before adding the batter so that
the batter begins to cook and
rise immediately.

Almond & Sesame Nut Roast

Toasted almonds are combined with sesame seeds, rice and vegetables in this tasty vegetarian roast. Serve with a delicious onion and mushroom sauce.

Serves 4

2 tbsp sesame or olive oil

1 small onion, chopped finely

60 g/2 oz risotto rice

300 ml/½ pint Fresh Vegetable Stock (see page 14)

1 large carrot, grated

1 large leek, trimmed and chopped finely

2 tsp sesame seeds, toasted

90 g/3 oz chopped almonds, toasted

60 g/2 oz ground almonds

90 g/3 oz mature Cheddar, grated

2 eggs, beaten

1 tsp dried mixed herbs

salt and pepper

sprigs of flat-leaf parsley, to garnish

fresh vegetables, to serve

SAUCE

25 g/1 oz butter

1 small onion, chopped finely

125 g/4½ oz mushrooms, chopped finely

25 g/1 oz plain flour

300 ml/½ pint Fresh Vegetable Stock (see page 14)

1 Heat the oil in a frying pan and fry the onion gently for 2–3 minutes. Add the rice and cook gently for 5–6 minutes, stirring frequently.

2 Add the vegetable stock, bring to the boil and then simmer for about 15 minutes, or until the rice is tender. Add a little extra water if necessary. Remove the pan from the heat and transfer the rice to a large bowl.

3 Add the carrot, leek, sesame seeds,

almonds, cheese, beaten eggs and herbs to the mixture. Mix well and season. Transfer the mixture to a greased 500 g/1 lb 2 oz loaf tin, levelling the surface. Bake in a preheated oven, 180°C/350°F/Gas Mark 4, for about 1 hour, or until set and firm. Leave in the tin for 10 minutes.

4 To make the sauce, melt the butter in a small saucepan and fry the onion until dark golden brown. Add the

mushrooms and cook for a further 2 minutes. Stir in the flour, cook gently for 1 minute and then gradually add the stock. Bring to the boil, stirring constantly, until thickened and blended. Season to taste.

5 Turn out the nut roast, slice and serve on warmed plates with fresh vegetables, accompanied by the sauce. Garnish with sprigs of flat-leaf parsley.

Green Vegetable Gougère

A tasty, simple supper dish of choux pastry and crisp green vegetables.
You can vary the vegetables according to taste.

Serves 4
150 g/5½ oz plain flour
125 g/4½ oz butter or vegetarian margarine
300 ml/½ pint water
4 eggs, beaten
90 g/3 oz grated Gruyère cheese
1 tbsp milk
salt and pepper

FILLING

25 g/1 oz garlic and herb butter or margarine
2 tsp olive oil
2 leeks, shredded
250 g/9 oz green cabbage, shredded finely
125 g/4½ oz bean-sprouts
½ tsp grated lime rind
1 tbsp lime juice
celery salt and pepper
lime slices, to garnish

1 Sift the flour on to a piece of baking parchment and set aside. Cut the butter or margarine into dice and put in a saucepan with the water. Heat until the butter has melted.

2 Bring the butter and water to the boil, then using the parchment as a funnel, shoot in the flour all at once. Beat until the mixture becomes thick. Remove from the heat and beat until the mixture is glossy and comes away from the sides of the saucepan.

3 Transfer to a bowl and cool for 10 minutes. Beat in the eggs, a little at a time, ensuring they are incorporated after each addition. Stir in 60 g/2 oz of the cheese and season.

4 Dampen a baking sheet. Place spoonfuls of the mixture in a 23 cm/9 inch circle on the baking sheet. Brush with milk and sprinkle with the cheese. Bake in a preheated oven, 220°C/425°F/Gas Mark 7, for 30–35 minutes until golden and crisp. Transfer to a serving plate.

5 Make the filling about 5 minutes before the end of cooking time. Heat the garlic butter or margarine and the oil in a frying pan and stir-fry the leeks and cabbage for 2 minutes.

6 Add the bean-sprouts, lime rind and juice and cook for 1 minute, stirring. Season with salt and pepper to taste, then pile into the centre of the cooked pastry ring. Garnish with lime slices and serve.

Filled Jacket Potatoes

Cook these potatoes conventionally, wrap them in foil and keep warm
at the edge of the barbecue, ready to fill with inspired mixtures.

Serves 4

4 large or 8 medium baking potatoes
paprika or chilli powder, or chopped
fresh herbs, to garnish

MEXICAN SWEETCORN RELISH

250 g/9 oz can sweetcorn, drained
$^1/_2$ red pepper deseeded
and chopped finely
5 cm/2 inch piece cucumber,
chopped finely
$^1/_2$ tsp chilli powder
salt and pepper

BLUE CHEESE, CELERY & CHIVE FILLING

125 g/4$^1/_2$ oz full-fat soft cheese
125 g/4$^1/_2$ oz natural fromage frais
125 g/4$^1/_2$ oz blue cheese, cut into cubes
1 celery stalk, chopped finely
2 tsp snipped fresh chives
celery salt and pepper

MUSHROOMS IN SPICY TOMATO SAUCE

30 g/1 oz butter or vegetarian margarine
250 g/9 oz button mushrooms
150 g/5$^1/_2$ oz natural yogurt
1 tbsp tomato purée
2 tsp mild curry powder
salt and pepper

1 Scrub the potatoes and prick them
with a fork. Bake in a preheated oven,
200°C/400°F/Gas Mark 6, for about 1
hour, or until just tender.

2 To make the Mexican Sweetcorn
Relish, put half of the sweetcorn
into a bowl. Put the remainder into
a blender or food processor for
10–15 seconds, or chop and mash

roughly by hand. Add the puréed
sweetcorn to the sweetcorn kernels
with the pepper, cucumber and chilli
powder. Season to taste.

3 To make the Blue Cheese, Celery &
Chive Filling, mix the soft cheese and
fromage frais together until smooth.
Add the blue cheese, celery and
chives. Season to taste with celery
salt and pepper.

4 To make the Mushrooms in Spicy
Tomato Sauce, melt the butter or
margarine in a small frying pan. Add
the mushrooms and cook gently for 3–4
minutes. Remove from the heat and stir
in the yogurt, tomato purée and curry
powder. Season.

5 Wrap the cooked potatoes in foil
and keep warm at the edge of the
barbecue. Serve the fillings sprinkled
with paprika or chilli powder or herbs.

Side Dishes
& Salads

An ideal accompaniment complements the main dish both visually and nutritionally. Many of the main dishes contained in this book will be rich in protein, therefore the side dishes in this chapter have been designed to be a little lighter in texture, while containing other important nutrients and lots of flavour and colour. The recipes contained within this chapter are perfect accompaniments for all occasions. A salad also makes a refreshing accompaniment to the main course. You could even serve two or three salads together as a complete meal – they are a good source of vitamins and minerals. Always use the freshest possible ingredients for maximum flavour and texture.

Pepperonata

A delicious mixture of peppers and onions, cooked
with tomatoes and herbs for a rich side dish.

Serves 4

4 tbsp olive oil

1 onion, halved and finely sliced

2 red peppers, cut into strips

2 green peppers, cut into strips

2 yellow peppers, cut into strips

2 garlic cloves, crushed

2 x 400 g/14 oz cans chopped
tomatoes, drained

2 tbsp chopped coriander

2 tbsp chopped pitted black olives

salt and pepper

1 Heat the oil in a large frying pan.
Add the onion and sauté for 5
minutes, stirring until just beginning
to colour.

2 Add the peppers and garlic
to the pan and cook for a further
3–4 minutes. Stir in the tomatoes
and coriander and season well. Cover
the pan and cook the vegetables
gently for about 30 minutes or until
the mixture is dry.

3 Stir in the olives and serve
immediately.

COOK'S TIP

Stir the vegetables occasionally during
the 30 minutes cooking time to prevent
them sticking to the bottom of the pan.
If the liquid has not evaporated by the
end of the cooking time, remove the lid
and boil rapidly until the dish is dry.

Cheese & Potato Layer Bake

This really is a great side dish, perfect for serving
with main meals cooked in the oven.

Serves 4
450 g/1 lb potatoes
1 leek, sliced
3 garlic cloves, crushed
50 g/1¾ oz Cheddar, grated
50 g/1¾ oz Mozzarella, grated
25 g/1 oz Parmesan cheese, grated
2 tbsp chopped parsley
150 ml/¼ pint single cream
150 ml/¼ pint milk
salt and pepper
freshly chopped flat-leaf parsley, to garnish

1 Cook the potatoes in a saucepan of boiling salted water for 10 minutes. Drain well. Cut the potatoes into thin slices. Arrange a layer of potatoes in the base of an ovenproof dish. Layer with a little of the leek, garlic, cheese and parsley. Season well.

2 Repeat the layers until all of the ingredients have been used, finishing with a layer of cheese on top.

3 Mix the cream and milk together, season and pour over the potato layers. Cook in a preheated oven, 160°C/325°F/Gas Mark 3, for 1–1¼ hours or until golden brown and bubbling and the potatoes are cooked through. Garnish and serve.

COOK'S TIP

Prepare the dish in advance, cover and chill for up to 12 hours until required.

Greek Green Beans

This dish contains many Greek flavours such as lemon, garlic, oregano and olives, for a really flavourful recipe.

Serves 4
400 g/14 oz can haricot beans, drained
1 tbsp olive oil
3 garlic cloves, crushed
450 ml/³/₄ pint vegetable stock
1 bay leaf
2 sprigs oregano
1 tbsp tomato purée
juice of 1 lemon
1 small red onion, chopped
25 g/1 oz pitted black olives, halved
salt and pepper

1 Put the haricot beans in a flameproof casserole dish.

2 Add the olive oil and garlic and cook over a gentle heat, stirring occasionally, for 4–5 minutes.

3 Add the stock, bay leaf, oregano, tomato purée, lemon juice and red onion, cover and simmer for about 1 hour or until the sauce has thickened.

4 Stir in the olives, season with salt and pepper to taste and serve.

COOK'S TIP

This dish may be made in advance and served cold with crusty bread, if preferred.

Cauliflower & Broccoli with Herb Sauce

Whole baby cauliflowers are used in this recipe. Try to find them if you can, if not use large bunches of florets.

Serves 4
2 baby cauliflowers
225 g/8 oz broccoli
salt and pepper

SAUCE
8 tbsp olive oil
4 tbsp butter
2 tsp grated root ginger
juice and rind of 2 lemons
5 tbsp chopped coriander
5 tbsp grated Cheddar

1 Cut the cauliflowers in half and the broccoli into very large florets. Cook the cauliflower and broccoli in a saucepan of boiling salted water for 10 minutes. Drain well and transfer to a shallow ovenproof dish.

2 To make the sauce, put the oil and butter in a pan and heat gently until the butter melts. Add the ginger, lemon juice and rind and coriander and simmer for 2–3 minutes.

3 Pour the sauce over the vegetables in the dish and sprinkle the cheese on top. Cook under a hot grill for 2–3 minutes or until the cheese is bubbling and serve immediately.

COOK'S VARIATION

Lime or orange could be used instead of the lemon for a fruity and refreshing sauce.

Pesto Potatoes

Pesto sauce is more commonly used as a pasta sauce but is
delicious served over potatoes as well.

Serves 4
900 g/2 lb small new potatoes
75 g/2³/₄ oz fresh basil
2 tbsp pine nuts
3 garlic cloves, crushed
100 ml/3¹/₂ fl oz olive oil
75 g/2³/₄ oz freshly grated Parmesan cheese and Pecorino cheese, mixed
salt and pepper
fresh basil sprigs, to garnish

1 Cook the potatoes in a saucepan of boiling salted water for 15 minutes or until tender. Drain well, transfer to a warm serving dish and keep warm.

2 Meanwhile, put the basil, pine nuts, garlic and a little salt and pepper to taste in a food processor. Blend for 30 seconds, adding the oil gradually, until smooth.

3 Remove the mixture from the food processor and stir in the cheeses.

4 Spoon the pesto sauce over the potatoes and mix well. Garnish with fresh basil sprigs and serve immediately.

COOK'S TIP

This sauce would also make a great salad dressing for a crisp green salad.

Sweet & Sour Aubergines

This is a dish of Persian origin, not Chinese as it sounds. Aubergines are fried and mixed with tomatoes, mint, sugar and vinegar for a really intense flavour.

Serves 4
2 large aubergines, cubed
6 tbsp olive oil
4 garlic cloves, crushed
1 onion, cut into eight
4 large tomatoes, seeded and chopped
3 tbsp chopped mint
150 ml/¼ pint vegetable stock
4 tsp brown sugar
2 tbsp red wine vinegar
1 tsp chilli flakes
salt and pepper
fresh mint sprigs, to garnish

1 Put the aubergines in a colander, sprinkle with salt and leave to stand for 30 minutes. Rinse under cold running water and drain well. Pat dry with absorbent kitchen paper.

2 Heat the oil in a large frying pan and sauté the aubergines, stirring constantly for 1–2 minutes.

3 Stir in the garlic and onion and cook for a further 2–3 minutes.

4 Stir in the tomatoes, mint and stock, cover and cook for 15–20 minutes or until the vegetables are tender.

5 Stir in the sugar, vinegar and chilli, season with salt and pepper to taste and cook for 2–3 minutes. Garnish with fresh mint sprigs and serve.

Spicy Lentils & Spinach

This is quite a filling dish, and should be
served with a light main course. Green split peas are a type of lentil.

Serves 4
225 g/8 oz green split peas
900 g/2 lb spinach
4 tbsp vegetable oil
1 onion, halved and sliced
1 tsp grated root ginger
1 tsp ground cumin
$\frac{1}{2}$ tsp chilli powder
$\frac{1}{2}$ tsp ground coriander
2 garlic cloves, crushed
300 ml/$\frac{1}{2}$ pint vegetable stock
salt and pepper
fresh coriander sprigs and lime wedges, to garnish

1 Rinse the peas under cold running water. Transfer to a mixing bowl, cover with cold water and leave to soak for 2 hours. Drain well.

2 Meanwhile, cook the spinach in a large saucepan for 5 minutes until wilted. Drain well and roughly chop.

3 Heat the oil in a large saucepan and sauté the onion, spices and garlic for 2–3 minutes, stirring well.

4 Add the lentils and spinach and stir in the stock. Cover and simmer for 10–15 minutes or until the lentils are cooked and the liquid has been absorbed. Season, garnish and serve.

COOK'S TIP

Once the lentils have been added, stir occasionally to prevent them from sticking to the pan.

Mini Vegetable Puff Pastry Cases

These are ideal with a more formal meal as they take
a little time to prepare and look really impressive.

Serves 4
450 g/1 lb puff pastry
1 egg, beaten
FILLING
225 g/8 oz sweet potato, cubed
100 g/3^{1}/$_{2}$ oz baby asparagus spears
2 tbsp butter
1 leek, sliced
2 small open-cup mushrooms, sliced
1 tsp lime juice
1 tsp chopped thyme
pinch of dried mustard
salt and pepper

1 Cut the pastry into four equal pieces. Roll each piece out on a lightly floured surface to form a 12.5 cm/ 5 inch square. Place on a dampened baking sheet and score a smaller 7.5 cm/2.5 inch square inside. Brush with beaten egg and cook in a preheated oven, 200°C/400°F/Gas Mark 6, for 20 minutes or until risen and golden brown.

2 Remove from the oven, then carefully cut out the central square of pastry, lift out and reserve.

3 To make the filling, cook the sweet potato in a saucepan of boiling water for 15 minutes, then drain well. Blanch the asparagus in a saucepan of boiling water for 10 minutes or until tender. Drain and reserve.

4 Melt the butter in a saucepan and sauté the leek and mushrooms for 2–3 minutes. Add the lime juice, thyme and mustard, season well and stir in the sweet potatoes and asparagus. Spoon into the pastry cases, top with the reserved pastry squares and serve immediately.

COOK'S TIP

Use a colourful selection of any vegetables you have to hand for this recipe.

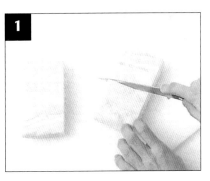

Steamed Vegetables with Vermouth

Serve these vegetables in their paper parcels to retain the juices.
The result is truly delicious.

Serves 4
1 carrot, cut into batons
1 fennel bulb, sliced
100 g/3¹/₂ oz courgettes, sliced
1 red pepper, sliced
4 small onions, halved
8 tbsp vermouth
4 tbsp lime juice
zest of 1 lime
pinch of paprika
4 sprigs tarragon
salt and pepper
fresh tarragon sprigs, to garnish

1 Place all of the vegetables in a large bowl and mix well.

2 Cut 4 large squares of greaseproof paper and place a quarter of the vegetables in the centre of each. Bring the sides of the paper up and pinch together to make an open parcel.

3 Mix the vermouth, lime juice, lime zest and paprika and pour a quarter of the mixture into each parcel. Season and add a tarragon sprig to each. Pinch the tops of the parcels together to seal.

4 Place the vegetable parcels in a steamer, cover and cook for 15–20 minutes or until the vegetables are tender. Garnish and serve.

COOK'S TIP

Seal the parcels well to prevent them opening during cooking and causing the juices to evaporate.

Soufflèd Cheesy Potato Fries

These small potato chunks are mixed in a creamy cheese sauce and
fried in oil until deliciously golden brown.

Serves 4

900 g/2 lb potatoes, cut into chunks
150 ml/¼ pint double cream
75 g/2¾ oz Gruyère cheese, grated
pinch of cayenne pepper
2 egg whites
oil, for deep-frying
salt and pepper
chopped flat-leaf parsley and grated
vegetarian cheese, to garnish

1 Cook the potatoes in a saucepan of
boiling salted water for 10 minutes.
Drain well and pat dry with absorbent
kitchen paper.

2 Mix the cream and cheese in a large
bowl. Stir in the cayenne pepper and
season to taste.

3 Whisk the egg whites until stiff
peaks form. Fold into the cheese
mixture until fully incorporated. Add
the potatoes, turning to coat.

4 Heat the oil for deep-frying to
180°C/350°F or until a cube of bread
browns in 30 seconds. Remove the
potatoes from the cheese mixture
with a slotted spoon and cook in the
oil, in batches, for 3–4 minutes or
until golden. Transfer to a serving
dish, garnish and serve.

COOK'S VARIATION

Add other flavourings, such as grated
nutmeg or curry powder, to the cream
and cheese.

Baked Celery with Cream & Pecans

This dish is topped with breadcrumbs for a crunchy topping, underneath
which is hidden a creamy celery and pecan mixture.

Serves 4
1 head of celery
1/2 tsp ground cumin
1/2 tsp ground coriander
1 garlic clove, crushed
1 red onion, thinly sliced
50 g/1³/₄ oz pecan nut halves
150 ml/¹/₄ pint vegetable stock
150 ml/¹/₄ pint single cream
50 g/1³/₄ oz fresh wholemeal breadcrumbs
25 g/1 oz Parmesan cheese, grated
salt and pepper
celery leaves, to garnish

1 Trim the celery and cut into matchsticks. Place the celery in an ovenproof dish with the ground cumin, coriander, garlic, onion and pecan nuts.

2 Mix the stock and cream together and pour over the vegetables. Season with salt and pepper to taste.

3 Mix the breadcrumbs and cheese together and sprinkle over the top to cover the vegetables. Cook in a preheated oven, 200°C/400°F/Gas Mark 6, for 40 minutes or until the vegetables are tender and the top crispy. Garnish with celery leaves and serve at once.

COOK'S VARIATION

You could use carrots or courgettes instead of the celery, if you prefer.

Beans in Lemon & Herb Sauce

Use a variety of beans if possible, although this recipe is
perfectly acceptable with just one type of bean.

Serves 4

900 g/2 lb mixed green beans,
such as broad beans,
French beans, runner beans

65 g/2½ oz butter or
vegetarian margarine

4 tsp plain flour

300 ml/½ pint vegetable stock

85 ml/3 fl oz dry white wine

6 tbsp single cream

3 tbsp chopped mixed herbs

2 tbsp lemon juice

zest of 1 lemon

salt and pepper

1 Cook the beans in a saucepan of
boiling salted water for 10 minutes or
until tender. Drain and place in a
warm serving dish.

2 Meanwhile, melt the butter in a
saucepan. Add the flour and cook for
1 minute. Remove the pan from the
heat and gradually stir in the stock
and wine. Return the pan to the heat
and bring to the boil.

3 Remove the pan from the heat once
again and stir in the cream, herbs,
lemon juice and rind. Season to taste.
Pour the sauce over the beans, mixing
well. Serve.

COOK'S TIP

Use a wide variety of herbs for flavour,
such as rosemary, thyme, tarragon and
sage.

Indian Spiced Potatoes & Spinach

This is a classic Indian accompaniment for
curries or plainer main vegetable dishes.

Serves 4
3 tbsp vegetable oil
1 red onion, sliced
2 garlic cloves, crushed
½ tsp chilli powder
2 tsp ground coriander
1 tsp ground cumin
150 ml/¼ pint vegetable stock
300 g/10½ oz potatoes, cubed
450 g/1 lb baby spinach
1 red chilli, sliced
salt and pepper

1 Heat the oil in a frying pan and
sauté the onion and garlic for
2–3 minutes, stirring. Stir in the chilli
powder, ground coriander and cumin
and cook for a further 30 seconds.

2 Add the stock, potato and spinach
and bring to the boil. Reduce the
heat, cover and simmer for about
10 minutes or until the potatoes are
cooked through.

3 Uncover, season, add the chilli and
cook for a further 2–3 minutes. Serve.

COOK'S VARIATION

Add other vegetables,
such as chopped tomatoes, for colour
and flavour.

Bulgar Pilau

Bulgar wheat is very easy to use and is a delicious alternative to rice,
having a distinctive nutty flavour.

Serves 4

75 g/2³/₄ oz butter or vegetarian
margarine

1 red onion, halved and sliced

2 garlic cloves, crushed

350 g/12 oz bulgar wheat

175 g/6 oz tomatoes, seeded
and chopped

50 g/1³/₄ oz baby corn cobs,
halved lengthwise

75 g/2³/₄ oz small broccoli florets

850 ml/1¹/₂ pints vegetable
stock

2 tbsp clear honey

50 g/1³/₄ oz sultanas

50 g/1³/₄ oz pine nuts

¹/₂ tsp ground cinnamon

¹/₂ tsp ground cumin

salt and pepper

sliced spring onions,
to garnish

1 Melt the butter or margarine in a
large flameproof casserole dish.

2 Add the onion and garlic and sauté
for 2–3 minutes, stirring occasionally.

3 Add the bulgar wheat, tomatoes,
corn cobs, broccoli and stock and
bring to the boil. Reduce the heat,
cover and cook for 15–20 minutes,
stirring occasionally.

4 Stir in the honey, sultanas, nuts,
ground cinnamon, cumin and salt and
pepper to taste, mixing well. Remove
the casserole from the heat, cover and
leave for 10 minutes.

5 Spoon the bulgar pilau into a warm
serving dish.

6 Garnish the bulgar pilau with sliced
spring onions and serve immediately.

COOK'S TIP

The dish is left to stand for 10 minutes in
order for the bulgar to finish cooking and
the flavours to mingle.

Aubergine & Courgette Galette

This is a dish of aubergine and courgettes layered with
a quick tomato sauce and melted cheese.

Serves 4
2 large aubergines, sliced
4 courgettes
2 x 400 g/14 oz cans chopped tomatoes, drained
2 tbsp tomato purée
2 garlic cloves, crushed
50 ml/2 fl oz olive oil
1 tsp caster sugar
2 tbsp chopped basil
olive oil, for frying
225 g/8 oz Mozzarella cheese, sliced
salt and pepper
fresh basil leaves, to garnish

1 Put the aubergine slices in a colander and sprinkle with salt. Leave to stand for 30 minutes, then rinse well under cold water and drain. Thinly slice the courgettes.

2 Meanwhile, put the tomatoes, tomato purée, garlic, olive oil, sugar and chopped basil into a pan and simmer for 20 minutes or until reduced by half. Season well.

3 Heat 2 tablespoons of olive oil in a large frying pan and cook the aubergine slices for 2–3 minutes until just beginning to brown. Remove from the pan.

4 Add a further 2 tablespoons of oil to the pan and fry the courgette slices until browned.

5 Lay half of the aubergine slices in the base of an ovenproof dish. Top with half of the tomato sauce and the courgettes and then half of the Mozzarella. Repeat the layers and bake in a preheated oven, 180°C/350°F/Gas Mark 4, for 45–50 minutes or until the vegetables are tender. Garnish with basil leaves and serve.

COOK'S TIP

Add a little more oil when frying the vegetables, if required and fry in batches to brown all of the slices evenly. The aubergine will absorb the oil quickly.

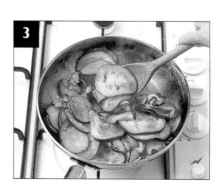

Courgette & Mint Salad

This salad uses lots of green-coloured ingredients which look and taste
wonderful with the minty yogurt dressing.

Serves 4
2 courgettes, cut into sticks
100 g/3¹/₂ oz French beans, cut into three
1 green pepper, cut into strips
2 celery sticks, sliced
1 bunch watercress

DRESSING

200 ml/7 fl oz natural yogurt
1 garlic clove, crushed
2 tbsp chopped mint
pepper

1 Cook the courgettes and beans in a
saucepan of salted boiling water for
7–8 minutes. Drain and leave to cool
completely.

2 Mix the vegetables with the pepper,
celery and watercress in a large bowl.

3 To make the dressing, mix the
yogurt, garlic, mint and pepper to
taste in a bowl.

4 Spoon the dressing on to the salad
and serve immediately.

COOK'S TIP

The salad must be served as soon as
the yogurt dressing has been added –
the dressing will start to separate if
kept for any length of time.

Alfalfa, Beetroot & Spinach Salad

This is a really refreshing salad that must be assembled just before serving
to prevent all of the ingredients being tainted pink by the beetroot.

Serves 4

100 g/3½ oz baby spinach
75 g/2¾ oz alfalfa sprouts
2 celery sticks, sliced
4 cooked beetroot, cut into eight

DRESSING

4 tbsp olive oil
1½ tbsp garlic wine vinegar
1 garlic clove, crushed
2 tsp clear honey
1 tbsp chopped chives

1 Place the spinach and alfalfa sprouts in a large bowl and mix together.

2 Add the celery and mix well.

3 Toss in the beetroot and mix well.

4 To make the dressing, mix the oil, wine vinegar, garlic, honey and chopped chives.

5 Pour the dressing over the salad, toss well and serve immediately.

COOK'S TIP

Alfalfa sprouts should be available from
most supermarkets, if not,
use beansprouts instead.

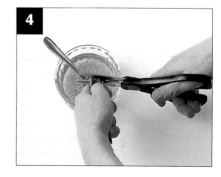

Moroccan Orange & Couscous Salad

Couscous is a type of semolina made from durum wheat. It is wonderful
in salads as it readily absorbs the flavour of the dressing.

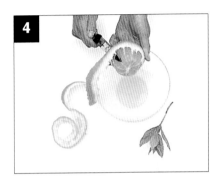

Serves 4–6

175 g/6 oz couscous

1 bunch spring onions,
trimmed and chopped finely

1 small green pepper, deseeded
and chopped

10 cm/4 inch piece cucumber,
chopped

175 g/6 oz can chick-peas,
rinsed and drained

60 g/2 oz sultanas
or raisins

2 oranges

salt and pepper

mixed salad leaves, to serve

sprigs of fresh mint, to garnish

DRESSING

finely grated rind of 1 orange

1 tbsp chopped fresh mint

150 ml/¼ pint
natural yogurt

1 Place the couscous in a large bowl,
cover with boiling water and leave
to soak for about 15 minutes or until
the grains have swelled. Stir with a
fork to separate the grains.

2 Add the spring onions, green
pepper, cucumber, chick-peas and
sultanas or raisins to the couscous,
stirring to combine. Season well with
salt and pepper.

3 To make the dressing, mix the
orange rind, mint and yogurt. Pour
over the couscous mixture and
stir well.

4 Using a sharp serrated knife,
remove the peel and pith from the
oranges.

5 Cut the orange flesh into segments,
removing all the membrane.

6 Arrange the lettuce leaves on
4 serving plates. Divide the couscous
mixture between the plates and
arrange the orange segments on top.
Garnish with sprigs of fresh mint
and serve.

Carrot & Cashew Nut Coleslaw

This simple salad has a dressing made from poppy seeds
pan-fried in sesame oil to bring out their flavour.

Serves 4
1 large carrot, grated
1 small onion, chopped finely
2 celery stalks, chopped
1/4 small, hard white cabbage, shredded
1 tbsp chopped fresh parsley
4 tbsp sesame oil
1/2 tsp poppy seeds
60 g/2 oz cashew nuts
2 tbsp white wine or cider vinegar
salt and pepper
chopped parsley, to garnish

1 In a large salad bowl, mix together the carrot, onion, celery and cabbage. Stir in the chopped parsley and season with salt and pepper.

2 Heat the sesame oil in a saucepan with a lid. Add the poppy seeds and cover the pan. Cook over a medium-high heat until the seeds start to make a popping sound. Remove from the heat and leave to cool.

3 Scatter the cashew nuts on to a baking sheet. Place them under a medium-hot grill and toast until lightly browned, being careful not to burn them. Leave to cool.

4 Add the vinegar to the oil and poppy seeds, mix well then pour over the carrot mixture. Add the cooled cashew nuts and toss together to coat with the dressing. Garnish the salad with sprigs of parsley and serve immediately.

Gado Gado

This is a very well known Indonesian salad of mixed
vegetables with a peanut dressing.

Serves 4
100 g/3^1/$_2$ oz white cabbage, shredded
100 g/3^1/$_2$ oz French beans, cut into 3
100 g/3^1/$_2$ oz carrots, cut into matchsticks
100 g/3^1/$_2$ oz cauliflower florets
100 g/3^1/$_2$ oz beansprouts

DRESSING

100 ml/3^1/$_2$ fl oz vegetable oil
100 g/3^1/$_2$ oz unsalted peanuts
2 garlic cloves, crushed
1 small onion, finely chopped
^{1}/$_2$ tsp chilli powder
^{1}/$_3$ tsp light brown sugar
425 ml/^{3}/$_4$ pint water
juice of ^{1}/$_2$ lemon
salt
sliced spring onions, to garnish

1 Cook the vegetables separately in a saucepan of salted boiling water for 4–5 minutes, drain well and chill.

2 To make the dressing, heat the oil in a frying pan and fry the peanuts for 3–4 minutes, turning. Remove from the pan with a slotted spoon and leave to drain on absorbent kitchen paper. Grind the peanuts in a blender or crush with a rolling pin until a fine mixture is formed.

3 Pour all but 1 tablespoon of oil from the pan and fry the garlic and onions for 1 minute. Add the chilli powder, sugar, a pinch of salt and the water and bring to the boil.

4 Stir in the peanuts. Reduce the heat and simmer for 4–5 minutes until the sauce thickens. Add the lemon juice and leave to cool.

5 Arrange the vegetables in a serving dish and spoon the peanut dressing into the centre. Garnish and serve.

COOK'S TIP

If necessary, you can prepare the peanut dressing in advance and then store it in the refrigerator for up to 12 hours before serving.

Salad with Garlic Yogurt Dressing

This is a very quick and refreshing salad using a whole range of colourful
ingredients which make it look as good as it tastes.

Serves 4

75 g/2³/₄ oz cucumber,
cut into sticks

6 spring onions, halved

2 tomatoes, seeded
and cut into eight

1 yellow pepper, cut into strips

2 celery sticks, cut into strips

4 radishes, quartered

75 g/2³/₄ oz rocket

1 tbsp chopped mint, to serve

DRESSING

2 tbsp lemon juice

1 garlic clove, crushed

150 ml/¹/₄ pint natural yogurt

2 tbsp olive oil

salt and pepper

1 Mix the cucumber, spring onions, tomatoes, pepper, celery, radishes and rocket together in a large serving bowl.

2 To make the dressing, stir the lemon juice, garlic, yogurt and oil together and season well.

3 Spoon the dressing over the salad and toss to mix. Sprinkle with chopped mint and serve.

COOK'S TIP

Do not toss the dressing into the salad until just before serving, otherwise it will turn soggy.

Three-Way Potato Salad

There's nothing to beat the flavour of new potatoes,
served just warm in a delicious dressing.

Serves 4

450 g/1 lb new potatoes, for each dressing
fresh herbs, to garnish
salt and pepper

LIGHT CURRY DRESSING

1 tbsp vegetable oil
1 tbsp medium curry paste
1 small onion, chopped
1 tbsp mango chutney, chopped
6 tbsp natural yogurt
3 tbsp single cream
2 tbsp mayonnaise
1 tbsp single cream, to garnish

VINAIGRETTE DRESSING

6 tbsp hazelnut oil
3 tbsp cider vinegar
1 tsp wholegrain mustard
1 tsp caster sugar
few basil leaves, torn into shreds

PARSLEY, SPRING ONION
& SOURED CREAM DRESSING

150 ml/¼ pint soured cream
3 tbsp light mayonnaise
4 spring onions,
trimmed and chopped finely
1 tbsp chopped fresh parsley

1 To make the Light Curry Dressing,
heat the vegetable oil in a frying pan.
Add the curry paste and onion and fry
together, stirring frequently, until the
onion is soft. Remove the pan from
the heat and leave to cool slightly.

2 Mix together the mango chutney,
yogurt, cream and mayonnaise. Add
the curry mixture and blend together.

Season to taste with salt and pepper.

3 To make the Vinaigrette Dressing,
whisk the hazelnut oil, cider vinegar,
mustard, sugar and basil together in a
small jug or bowl. Season with salt and
pepper to taste.

4 To make the Parsley, Spring Onion
and Soured Cream Dressing, combine
all the ingredients, mixing well.

Season to taste with salt and pepper.

5 Cook the potatoes in a pan of lightly
salted boiling water until just tender.
Drain and leave to cool for 5 minutes.
Add the chosen dressing, tossing to
coat. Serve, garnished with fresh
herbs, spooning a little single cream
on to the potatoes if you have used
the curry dressing.

Bean, Avocado & Tomato Salad

This is a colourful salad with a Mexican theme, using beans, tomatoes and avocado.
The chilli dressing adds a little kick.

Serves 4
lollo rosso lettuce
2 ripe avocados
2 tsp lemon juice
4 medium tomatoes
1 onion
175 g/6 oz mixed canned beans, drained
DRESSING
4 tbsp olive oil
drop of chilli oil
2 tbsp garlic wine vinegar
pinch of caster sugar
pinch of chilli powder
1 tbsp chopped parsley

1 Line a serving bowl with the lettuce. Thinly slice the avocados and sprinkle with lemon juice.

2 Thinly slice the tomato and onion. Arrange the avocado, tomatoes and onion around the salad bowl, leaving a space in the centre.

3 Spoon the beans into the centre of the salad and whisk the dressing ingredients together. Pour the dressing over the salad and serve.

COOK'S TIP

The lemon juice is sprinkled on to the avocados to prevent discoloration when in contact with the air. For this reason the salad should be prepared, assembled and served quite quickly.

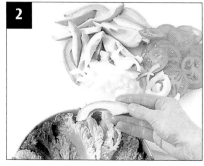

Grilled Vegetables with Mustard Dressing

The vegetables for this dish are best prepared well
in advance and chilled before serving.

Serves 4

1 courgette, sliced
1 yellow pepper, sliced
1 aubergine, sliced
1 fennel bulb, cut into eight
1 red onion, cut into eight
16 cherry tomatoes
3 tbsp olive oil
1 garlic clove, crushed
fresh rosemary sprigs, to garnish

DRESSING

4 tbsp olive oil
2 tbsp balsamic vinegar
2 tsp chopped rosemary
1 tsp Dijon mustard
1 tsp clear honey
2 tsp lemon juice

1 Put all of the vegetables except for the cherry tomatoes on to a baking sheet.

2 Mix the oil and garlic and brush over the vegetables. Cook under a medium-hot grill for 10 minutes until tender and beginning to char. Leave to cool. Spoon the vegetables into a serving bowl.

3 Mix the dressing ingredients and pour over the vegetables. Cover and chill for 1 hour. Garnish and serve.

COOK'S TIP

This dish could also be served warm – heat the dressing in a pan and then toss into the vegetables.

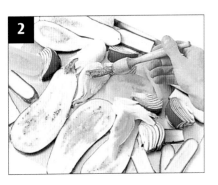

Red Cabbage & Pear Salad

Red cabbage is much underused – it is a colourful and tasty ingredient
which is perfect with fruits, such as pears or apples.

Serves 4

350 g/12 oz red cabbage,
finely shredded

2 Conference pears,
thinly sliced

4 spring onions, sliced

1 carrot, grated

fresh chives, to garnish

lollo biondo leaves, to serve

DRESSING

4 tbsp pear juice

1 tsp wholegrain mustard

3 tbsp olive oil

1 tbsp garlic wine vinegar

1 tbsp chopped chives

1 Toss the cabbage, pears and spring
onions together.

2 Line a serving dish with lettuce
leaves and spoon the cabbage and
pear mixture into the centre.

3 Sprinkle the carrot into the centre
of the cabbage to form a domed pile.

4 To make the dressing, mix the pear
juice, mustard, oil, wine vinegar and
chives together. Pour the dressing
over the salad, garnish and serve
immediately.

COOK'S TIP

Mix the salad just before serving
to prevent the colour from the red
cabbage bleeding into the
other ingredients.

Three Bean Salad

Fresh dwarf green beans are combined with soya beans and
red kidney beans in a chive and tomato dressing to make a tasty salad.

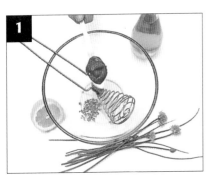

Serves 4-6

3 tbsp olive oil

1 tbsp lemon juice

1 tbsp tomato purée

1 tbsp light malt vinegar

1 tbsp chopped fresh chives

175 g/6 oz dwarf green beans

400 g/14 oz can soya beans,
rinsed and drained

400 g/14 oz can red kidney beans,
rinsed and drained

2 tomatoes, chopped

4 spring onions,
trimmed and chopped

125 g/4½ oz Feta cheese,
cut into cubes

salt and pepper

mixed salad leaves,
to serve

chopped fresh chives,
to garnish

1 Put the olive oil, lemon juice,
tomato purée, vinegar and chives into
a large bowl and whisk together until
thoroughly combined.

2 Cook the dwarf green beans in a
little boiling, lightly salted water until
just cooked, about 4–5 minutes.
Drain, refresh under cold running
water and drain again. Pat dry with
paper towels.

COOK'S VARIATION

Try haricot beans or black-eye beans
instead of the soya beans and red
kidney beans.

3 Add the green beans, soya beans
and red kidney beans to the dressing,
stirring to mix.

4 Add the tomatoes, spring onions
and Feta cheese to the bean mixture,
tossing gently to coat in the dressing.

Season well with salt and pepper to
taste.

5 Arrange the mixed salad leaves on
4 serving plates. Transfer the bean
salad to serving plates and garnish
with chopped chives.

Marinated Vegetable Salad

Lightly steamed vegetables taste superb served slightly warm in a marinade
of olive oil, white wine, vinegar and fresh herbs.

Serves 4-6

175 g/6 oz baby carrots, trimmed

2 celery hearts, cut into 4 pieces

125g/4^1/$_2$ oz sugar snap peas
or mangetout

1 fennel bulb, sliced

175 g/6 oz small asparagus spears

15 g/^{1}/$_2$ oz
sunflower seeds

sprigs of fresh dill, to garnish

DRESSING

4 tbsp olive oil

4 tbsp dry white wine

2 tbsp white wine vinegar

1 tbsp chopped fresh dill

1 tbsp chopped fresh parsley

salt and pepper

1 Steam the carrots, celery, sugar
snap peas or mangetout, fennel and
asparagus over a pan of gently boiling
water until just tender. It is important
that they retain a little 'bite'.

2 Meanwhile, make the dressing. Mix
together the olive oil, wine, vinegar
and chopped herbs. Season well with
salt and pepper.

3 When the vegetables are cooked,
transfer to a serving dish and pour
over the dressing at once. The hot
vegetables will absorb the flavour of
the dressing as they cool.

4 Scatter the sunflower seeds on to a
baking sheet and toast them under a
preheated grill until lightly browned.
Sprinkle them over the vegetables.

5 Serve the salad while the vegetables
are still slightly warm, garnished with
sprigs of fresh dill.

COOK'S VARIATION

Sesame seeds or pine nuts can be used
instead of sunflower seeds for
sprinkling over the vegetables.

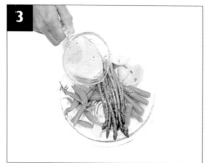

Goat's Cheese with Walnuts in Oil & Vinegar Dressing

This delicious salad combines soft goat's cheese with walnut halves,
served on a bed of mixed salad leaves.

Serves 4

90 g/3 oz walnut halves
mixed salad leaves
125 g/4¹/₂ oz soft goat's cheese
snipped fresh chives, to garnish

DRESSING

6 tbsp walnut oil
3 tbsp white wine vinegar
1 tbsp clear honey
1 tsp Dijon mustard
pinch of ground ginger
salt and pepper

1 To make the dressing, whisk together the walnut oil, wine vinegar, honey, mustard and ginger in a small saucepan. Season to taste.

2 Heat the dressing gently, stirring occasionally, until warm. Add the walnut halves and continue to heat for 3–4 minutes.

3 Arrange the salad leaves on 4 serving plates and place spoonfuls of goat's cheese on top. Lift the walnut halves from the dressing with a perforated spoon, and scatter them over the salad.

4 Transfer the warm dressing to a small jug. Sprinkle chives over the salads and serve with the dressing.

COOK'S VARIATION

Use hazelnut oil and hazelnuts rather than walnut oil and walnuts.

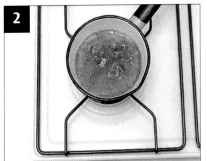

Desserts

Vegetarian or not, confirmed pudding lovers feel disappointed if there isn't a tempting dessert to finish off a good meal. Desserts help satisfy a deep-seated desire for something sweet, but they are often loaded with fat and sugar which are notorious for piling on the calories.

The recipes in this chapter offer the ideal solution. They are light but full of flavour, so you can still enjoy that sweet treat without the bulging waistline and distended feeling at the end of a meal. This is particularly important after a vegetarian meal as the food can often be quite filling.

A lot of the recipes are based on fruit, which is the perfect ingredient for healthy desserts that are every bit as tempting as those based on lavish amounts of cream and butter. We've also included one or two indulgences such as Boston Chocolate Pie and Chocolate Mousse.

Berry Cheesecake

Use a mixture of berries, such as blueberries, blackberries,
raspberries and strawberries, for a really fruity cheesecake.

Serves 8
BASE
75 g/2³⁄₄ oz vegetarian margarine
175 g/6 oz oatmeal biscuits
50 g/1³⁄₄ oz desiccated coconut
TOPPING
1¹⁄₂ tsp gelazone
125 ml/4 fl oz evaporated milk
1 egg
6 tbsp light brown sugar
450 g/1 lb soft cream cheese
350 g/12 oz mixed berries
2 tbsp clear honey

1 Put the margarine in a saucepan
and heat until melted. Put the biscuits
in a food processor and blend until
smooth or crush finely with a rolling
pin. Stir into the margarine with the
coconut. Press the mixture into a
base-lined 20 cm/8 inch spring-form
tin and chill in the refrigerator whilst
preparing the filling.

2 To make the topping, sprinkle the
gelazone over 9 tbsp of cold water and
stir to dissolve. Bring to the boil and
boil for 2 minutes. Let cool slightly.

3 Put the milk, egg, sugar and soft
cream cheese in a bowl and beat until
smooth. Stir in 50 g/1³⁄₄ oz of the
berries. Stir in the gelazone in a
stream, stirring constantly.

4 Spoon the mixture on to the biscuit
base and return to the refrigerator for
2 hours or until set.

5 Remove the cheesecake from the tin
and transfer to a serving plate.
Arrange the remaining berries on top
of the cheesecake and drizzle the
honey over the top. Serve.

COOK'S TIP

Warm the honey slightly to make
it runnier and easier to drizzle.

Apricot Brûlée

Serve this delicious dessert with crisp-baked meringues
for an extra-special occasion.

Serves 4
125 g/4^{1}/$_{2}$ oz unsulphured dried apricots
150 ml/^{1}/$_{4}$ pint orange juice
4 egg yolks
2 tbsp caster sugar
150 ml/^{1}/$_{4}$ pint natural yogurt
150 ml/^{1}/$_{4}$ pint double cream
1 tsp vanilla flavouring
90 g/3 oz demerara sugar
meringues, to serve (optional)

1 Place the apricots in a bowl. Pour the orange juice over the apricots and leave to soak for at least 1 hour. Pour into a small pan, bring slowly to the boil and simmer for 20 minutes. Purée in a blender or food processor, or chop very finely and push through a sieve.

2 Beat together the egg yolks and sugar until the mixture is light and fluffy. Place the yogurt in a small pan, add the cream and vanilla and bring to the boil over a low heat.

3 Pour the yogurt mixture over the eggs, beating all the time, then transfer to the top of a double boiler, or place the bowl over a pan of simmering water. Stir until the custard thickens.

4 Divide the apricot mixture between 6 ramekins and spoon the custard on top. Cool, then chill in the refrigerator.

5 Preheat the grill to high. Sprinkle the demerara sugar over the custard and grill until the sugar caramelizes. Set aside to cool.

6 To serve the apricot brûlée, crack the hard caramel topping with the back of a tablespoon. Serve with the meringues, if using.

Cherry Pancakes

This dish can be made with either fresh pitted cherries or canned cherries for speed.

Serves 4
FILLING
400 g/14 oz can pitted cherries, plus juice
$^{1}/_{2}$ tsp almond essence
$^{1}/_{2}$ tsp mixed spice
2 tbsp cornflour
PANCAKES
100 g/3$^{1}/_{2}$ oz plain flour
pinch of salt
2 tbsp chopped mint
1 egg
300 ml/$^{1}/_{2}$ pint milk
vegetable oil, for frying
icing and toasted
flaked almonds, to decorate

1 Put the cherries and 300 ml/$^{1}/_{2}$ pint of the juice in a pan with the almond essence and mixed spice. Stir in the cornflour and bring to the boil, stirring until thickened and clear. Set aside.

2 To make the pancakes, sieve the flour into a bowl with the salt. Add the chopped mint and make a well in the centre. Gradually beat in the egg and milk to make a smooth batter.

3 Heat 1 tbsp of oil in an 18 cm/ 7 inch frying pan; pour off the oil when hot. Add just enough batter to coat the base of the frying pan and cook for 1–2 minutes or until the underside is cooked. Flip the pancake over and cook for 1 minute. Remove from the pan and keep warm. Heat 1 tbsp of the oil in the pan again and repeat to use up all the batter.

4 Spoon a quarter of the cherry filling on to a quarter of each pancake and fold the pancake into a cone shape. Dust with icing sugar and sprinkle the flaked almonds over the top. Serve.

COOK'S VARIATION

Use other fillings, such as gooseberries or blackberries, as an alternative to the cherries.

Raspberry Fool

This dish is very easy to make and can be made in advance
and stored in the refrigerator.

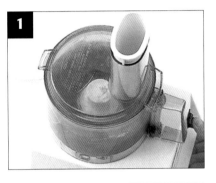

Serves 4

300 g/10$^{1}/_{2}$ oz fresh raspberries

50 g/1$^{3}/_{4}$ oz icing sugar

$^{1}/_{2}$ tsp vanilla essence

300 ml/$^{1}/_{2}$ pint crème fraîche,
plus extra to decorate

2 egg whites

raspberries and lemon balm leaves,
to decorate

1 Put the raspberries and icing sugar
in a food processor or blender and
blend until smooth.

2 Put the vanilla essence and crème
fraîche (reserving 1 tablespoon per
portion for decorating) in a bowl and
stir in the raspberry mixture.

3 Whisk the egg whites in a separate
mixing bowl until stiff peaks form
and fold into the raspberry mixture
until fully incorporated.

4 Spoon the raspberry fool into
serving dishes and chill for at least
1 hour. Decorate and serve.

COOK'S VARIATION

This recipe is also delicious made with
strawberries or blackberries.

Steamed Coffee Sponge & Sauce

This sponge pudding is very light and is delicious
with a coffee or chocolate sauce.

Serves 4
2 tbsp vegetarian margarine
2 tbsp soft brown sugar
2 eggs
50 g/1³/₄ oz plain flour
³/₄ tsp baking powder
6 tbsp milk
1 tsp coffee flavouring
SAUCE
300 ml/¹/₂ pint milk
1 tbsp soft brown sugar
1 tsp cocoa powder
2 tbsp cornflour

1 Lightly grease a 600 ml/1 pint heatproof pudding basin. Cream the margarine and sugar until light and fluffy and beat in the eggs.

2 Gradually stir in the flour and baking powder and then the milk and coffee flavouring to make a smooth batter.

3 Spoon the mixture into the prepared pudding basin and cover with a pleated piece of greaseproof paper and then a pleated piece of foil, securing around the bowl with string. Place in a steamer or large pan and half fill with boiling water. Cover and steam for 1–1¼ hours or until cooked through.

4 To make the sauce, put the milk, sugar and cocoa powder in a pan and heat until the sugar dissolves. Blend the cornflour with 4 tablespoons of cold water to make a

paste and stir into the pan. Bring to the boil, stirring until thickened. Cook over a gentle heat for 1 minute.

5 Turn the pudding out on to a serving plate and spoon the sauce over the top. Serve.

COOK'S TIP

The pudding is covered with pleated paper and foil to allow it to rise. The foil will react with the steam and must therefore not be placed directly against the pudding.

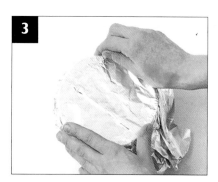

Lemon & Lime Syllabub

This dessert is rich but absolutely delicious. It is not, however, for the
calorie conscious as it contains a high proportion of cream,
but it's well worth blowing the diet for!

Serves 4
50 g/1³/₄ oz caster sugar
grated zest and juice of 1 small lemon
grated zest and juice of 1 small lime
50 ml/2 fl oz Marsala or medium sherry
300 ml/¹/₂ pint double cream
lime and lemon zest, to decorate

1 Put the sugar, fruit juices and zest and sherry in a bowl, mix well and leave to infuse for 2 hours.

2 Add the cream to the mixture and whisk until it just holds its shape.

3 Spoon the mixture into 4 tall serving glasses and chill in the refrigerator for 2 hours before decorating and serving.

COOK'S TIP

Serve with almond biscuits or uncoated florentines. Do not overwhip the cream when adding to the lemon and lime mixture as it may curdle.

Warm Currants in Cassis

Crème de cassis is a blackcurrant-based liqueur which comes
from France and is an excellent flavouring for fruit dishes.

Serves 4
350 g/12 oz blackcurrants
250 g/9 oz redcurrants
4 tbsp caster sugar
grated rind and juice of 1 orange
2 tsp arrowroot
2 tbsp crème de cassis
fresh mint leaves, to decorate
whipped cream, to serve

1 Using a fork, strip the currants from their stalks and place in a saucepan.

2 Add the sugar and orange rind and juice, and heat gently until the sugar has dissolved. Bring to the boil and simmer gently for 5 minutes.

3 Strain the currants and place in a bowl. Return the juice to the pan.

4 Blend the arrowroot with a little water. Mix the arrowroot into the juice then boil until thickened.

5 Leave to cool slightly, then stir in the cassis.

6 Serve in individual dishes with whipped cream.

Cherry Clafoutis

This is a hot dessert that is simple and quick to put together. Try the batter with other fruits – apricots and plums are particularly delicious.

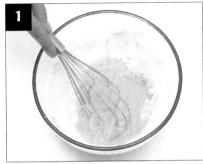

Serves 6
125 g/4¹/₂ oz plain flour
4 eggs, lightly beaten
2 tbsp caster sugar
pinch of salt
600 ml/1 pint milk
butter, for greasing
500 g/1 lb 2 oz black cherries, fresh or canned, pitted
3 tbsp brandy
1 tbsp sugar, to decorate

1 Sift the flour into a large bowl. Make a well in the centre and add the eggs, sugar and salt. Draw in the flour from around the edges and whisk.

2 Pour in the milk and whisk the batter thoroughly until very smooth.

3 Lightly grease a 1.75 litre/3 pint ovenproof serving dish and pour in half of the batter.

4 Spoon in the cherries and pour the remaining batter over the top. Sprinkle the brandy over the batter.

5 Bake in a preheated oven, 180°C/350°F/Gas Mark 4, for 40 minutes.

6 Remove from the oven and sprinkle with the sugar just before serving. Serve warm.

Cinnamon Pears with Maple & Ricotta Cream

These spicy yet sweet pears are accompanied by a delicious melt-in-the-mouth cream, which is relatively low in fat.

Serves 4
1 lemon
4 firm ripe pears
1 cinnamon stick, broken in half
300 ml/$^1/_2$ pint dry cider
or unsweetened apple juice
fresh mint leaves, to decorate

MAPLE RICOTTA CREAM

125 g/4$^1/_2$ oz
medium-fat Ricotta
125 g/4$^1/_2$ oz low-fat natural
fromage frais
$^1/_2$ tsp ground cinnamon
$^1/_2$ tsp grated lemon rind
1 tbsp maple syrup
grated lemon rind, to decorate

1 Using a vegetable peeler, remove the rind from the lemon and place in a non-stick frying pan. Squeeze the lemon and pour the juice into a shallow bowl.

2 Peel, halve and core the pears. Place in a bowl and toss in the lemon juice to prevent discoloration. Add to the frying pan and pour over the lemon juice remaining in the bowl.

3 Add the cinnamon stick and cider or apple juice. Bring to the boil, then lower the heat and simmer for 10 minutes. Remove the pears using a slotted spoon, reserving the cooking juice.

4 Put the pears in a warm heatproof serving dish, cover with foil and keep warm in a preheated oven at 110°C/ 225°F/Gas Mark $^1/_4$.

5 Return the pan to the heat, bring to the boil, then simmer for 8–10 minutes until reduced by half. Spoon the syrup over the pears.

6 To make the maple Ricotta cream, mix together all the ingredients. Decorate with lemon rind and serve with the pears.

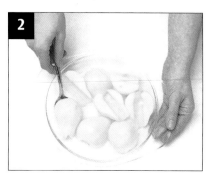

Blackberry, Apple & Fresh Fig Compôte

Elderflower cordial is used in the syrup for this refreshing fruit compôte, giving it a delightfully summery flavour.

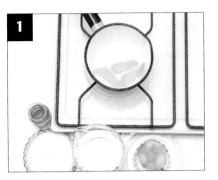

Serves 4

1 lemon
60 g/2 oz caster
sugar
4 tbsp elderflower cordial
300 ml/½ pint water
4 dessert apples
250 g/9 oz/2 cups blackberries
2 fresh figs

SAUCE

150 g/5½ oz thick
natural yogurt
2 tbsp clear honey

1 Pare the rind from the lemon, using a potato peeler. Squeeze the juice. Put the lemon rind and juice into a saucepan with the sugar, elderflower cordial and water. Heat gently and simmer, uncovered, for 10 minutes.

2 Core and slice the apples, then add them to the saucepan. Simmer gently for 4–5 minutes or until just tender. Leave to cool.

3 Transfer the apples and syrup to a serving bowl and add the blackberries. Slice the figs and add to the bowl, stirring gently to mix. Cover and chill until ready to serve.

4 To make the sauce, spoon the yogurt into a small serving bowl and drizzle the honey over the top. Cover and chill before serving.

Autumn Fruit Bread Pudding

This is like a summer pudding, but it uses fruits which appear later in the year,
such as apples, pears and blackberries, as a succulent filling.

Serves 8

900 g/2 lb mixed blackberries,
chopped apples, chopped pears

150 g/5½ oz soft light brown sugar

1 tsp cinnamon

225 g/8 oz white bread,
thinly sliced, crusts removed

1 Place the fruit in a large saucepan
with the sugar, cinnamon and 100 ml/
3½ fl oz of water, stir and bring to the
boil. Reduce the heat and simmer for
5–10 minutes so that the fruits soften
but still hold their shape.

2 Meanwhile, line the base and sides
of a 850 ml/1½ pint pudding basin
with the bread slices, ensuring that
there are no gaps between the pieces
of bread.

3 Spoon the fruit into the centre of
the bread-lined bowl and cover the
fruit with the remaining bread.

4 Place a saucer on top of the bread
and weight it down. Leave to chill in
the refrigerator overnight.

5 Turn the pudding out on to a
serving plate and serve immediately.

COOK'S TIP

Stand the pudding on a plate when
chilling to catch any juices that run
down the sides of the basin.

Green Fruit Salad with Mint & Lemon Syrup

This delightful fresh fruit salad is the perfect finale for a summer barbecue.
It has a lovely light syrup made with fresh mint and honey.

Serves 4

1 small Charentais or honeydew melon
2 green apples
2 kiwi fruit
125 g/4$^{1}/_{2}$ oz seedless white grapes
fresh mint sprigs, to decorate

SYRUP

1 lemon
150 ml/$^{1}/_{4}$ pint white wine
150 ml/$^{1}/_{4}$ pint water
4 tbsp clear honey
few sprigs of fresh mint

1 To make the syrup, pare the rind from the lemon, using a potato peeler.

2 Put the lemon rind in a saucepan with the wine, water and honey. Bring to the boil, then simmer gently for 10 minutes. Remove from the heat. Add the sprigs of mint and leave to cool.

3 Slice the melon in half and scoop out the seeds. Using a melon baller or a teaspoon, scoop out melon balls.

4 Core and chop the apples. Peel and slice the kiwi fruit.

5 Strain the cooled syrup into a serving bowl, removing and reserving the lemon rind and discarding the mint sprigs. Add the apple, grapes, kiwi and melon. Stir through gently to mix.

6 Decorate with sprigs of fresh mint and some of the reserved lemon rind and serve.

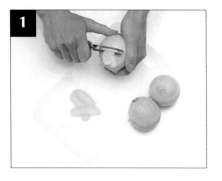

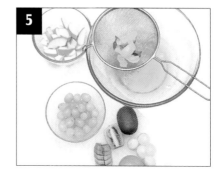

Chocolate Mousse

This is a light and fluffy, but fruity-tasting mousse which
is delicious with a fresh fruit sauce.

Serves 8

100 g/3½ oz dark chocolate, melted
300 ml/½ pint natural yogurt
150 ml/¼ pint quark
4 tbsp caster sugar
1 tbsp orange juice
1 tbsp brandy
1½ tsp gelazone
2 large egg whites
coarsely grated dark and white chocolate
and orange zest, to decorate

1 Put the chocolate, yogurt, quark, sugar, orange juice and brandy in a food processor and blend for 30 seconds. Transfer to a mixing bowl.

2 Sprinkle the gelazone over 9 tbsp of cold water and stir until dissolved. Bring to the boil and boil for 2 minutes. Leave to cool slightly, then stir into the chocolate mixture.

3 Whisk the egg whites until peaking and fold into the chocolate mixture.

4 Line a 900 ml/1½ pint loaf tin with cling film. Spoon the mousse into the tin. Chill for 2 hours until set. Turn the mousse out on to a plate, decorate and serve.

COOK'S TIP

For a quick fruit sauce, blend a can of mandarin segments in natural juice in a food processor and press through a sieve. Stir in 1 tbsp clear honey and serve with the mousse.

Apple Fritters & Almond Sauce

These apple fritters are coated in a light, spiced batter
and deep-fried until crisp and golden. Serve warm.

Serves 4
100 g/3¹/₂ oz plain flour
pinch of salt
¹/₂ tsp ground cinnamon
12 tbsp warm water
4 tsp vegetable oil
2 egg whites
2 dessert apples, peeled
vegetable or sunflower oil, for deep-frying
caster sugar and cinnamon,
to serve

SAUCE

150 ml/¹/₄ pint natural yogurt
¹/₂ tsp vanilla essence
2 tsp clear honey

1 Sieve the flour and salt into a
mixing bowl.

2 Add the cinnamon and mix well.
Stir in the water and oil to make a
smooth batter.

3 Whisk the egg whites until stiff
peaks form and fold into the batter.

4 Cut the apples into chunks and
dip the pieces of apple into the batter
to coat.

5 Heat the oil for deep-frying to
180°C/350°F or until a cube of bread
browns in 30 seconds. Fry the apple
pieces, in batches, for 3–4 minutes
until golden brown and puffy.
Remove the apple fritters from the oil
with a slotted spoon and leave to
drain on absorbent kitchen paper.

6 Mix the caster sugar and cinnamon
and sprinkle over the fritters.

7 Mix the sauce ingredients in a serving
bowl and serve with the fritters.

COOK'S VARIATION

Use pieces of banana or pineapple
instead of the apple, if you prefer.

Mixed Fruit Crumble

I have used tropical fruits in this crumble, flavoured with ginger and coconut, for something a little different and very tasty.

Serves 4
2 mangoes, sliced
1 paw paw, seeded and sliced
225 g/8 oz fresh pineapple, cubed
1½ tsp ground ginger
100 g/3½ oz vegetarian margarine
100 g/3½ oz soft light brown sugar
175 g/6 oz plain flour
50 g/1¾ oz desiccated coconut, plus extra to decorate

1 Place the fruit in a pan with ½ tsp of the ginger. 25 g/1 oz of the margarine and 50 g/1¾ oz of the sugar. Cook over a gentle heat for 10 minutes until the fruit softens. Spoon the fruit into the base of a shallow ovenproof dish.

2 Mix the flour and remaining ginger together. Rub in the remaining margarine until the mixture resembles fine breadcrumbs. Stir in the remaining sugar and the coconut and spoon over the fruit to cover completely.

3 Cook the crumble in a preheated oven at 180°C/350°F/Gas Mark 4 for about 40 minutes or until the top is crisp. Decorate and serve.

COOK'S VARIATION

Use other fruits, such as plums, apples or blackberries, as a fruit base and add chopped nuts to the topping instead of the coconut.

Boston Chocolate Pie

This lighter version of the popular chocolate cream pie
is made with yogurt and crème fraîche.

Serves 6
250 g/9 oz shortcrust pastry
250 g/9 oz dark chocolate
150 ml/¼ pint crème fraîche

FILLING

3 eggs
125 g/4½ oz caster sugar
60 g/2 oz flour,
plus extra for dusting
1 tbsp icing sugar, plus extra to decorate
pinch of salt
1 tsp vanilla flavouring
400 ml/14 fl oz milk
150 ml/¼ pint natural yogurt
150 g/5½ oz dark chocolate,
broken into pieces
2 tbsp kirsch

1 Roll out the pastry and use to line a 23 cm/9 inch loose-bottomed flan tin. Prick the base with a fork, line with baking parchment, fill with baking beans and bake blind in a preheated oven, 200°C/400°F/Gas Mark 6, for 20 minutes. Remove the beans and parchment and return to the oven for 5 minutes. Cool on a wire rack.

2 To make the Chocolate Caraque, melt the chocolate in a heatproof bowl set over a pan of simmering water. Spread on to a cool surface with a palette knife. When cool, scrape it into curls by drawing a sharp knife firmly across the surface.

3 To make the filling, beat the eggs and sugar until fluffy. Sieve the flour, icing sugar and salt over the beaten eggs and stir until blended. Stir in the vanilla flavouring. Put the milk and yogurt in a small pan, bring slowly to the boil, then strain into the egg mixture. Pour into the top of a double boiler, or a bowl set over a pan of simmering water, and stir until thick enough to coat the back of a spoon. Melt the chocolate and kirsch over a low heat. When it has melted, stir into the custard. Remove the

custard from the heat and stand the double boiler or bowl in cold water to prevent further cooking. Leave to cool.

4 Pour the chocolate filling into the pastry case. Spread the crème fraîche over the chocolate, and arrange the caraque on top.

Fruit Brûlée

This is a cheat's brûlée, in that yogurt is used to cover a base of fruit,
before being sprinkled with sugar and grilled.

Serves 4
4 plums, stoned and sliced
2 cooking apples, peeled and sliced
1 tsp ground ginger
600 ml/1 pint Greek-style yogurt
2 tbsp icing sugar, sieved
1 tsp almond essence
75 g/2¾ oz demerara sugar

1 Put the plums and apples in a saucepan with 2 tablespoons of water and cook for 7–10 minutes until tender but not mushy. Leave to cool, then stir in the ginger. Using a slotted spoon, spoon the mixture into the base of a shallow serving dish.

2 Mix the yogurt, icing sugar and almond essence together and spoon on to the fruit.

3 Sprinkle the demerara sugar over the top of the yogurt and cook under a hot grill for 3–4 minutes or until the sugar has dissolved and formed a crust. Chill in the refrigerator for 1 hour and serve.

COOK'S TIP

Use any variety of fruit, such as mixed berries or mango pieces, for this dessert, but do not poach them.

Pear Cake

This is a really moist cake, flavoured with chopped pears and almond.

Serves 12

4 pears, peeled

100 g/3¹⁄₂ oz soft light brown sugar

4 tbsp milk

200 g/7 oz plain flour

2 tsp baking powder

2 tbsp clear honey, plus extra
to drizzle

2 tsp ground cinnamon

2 egg whites

1 Grease and line the base of a 20 cm/
8 inch cake tin.

2 Put 1 pear in a food processor with
2 tablespoons of water and blend
until almost smooth. Transfer to a
mixing bowl.

3 Sieve in the flour and baking
powder. Beat in the sugar, milk,
honey and cinnamon and mix well.

4 Chop all but one of the remaining
pears and add to the mixture.

5 Whisk the egg whites until stiff
peaks form and gently fold into the
mixture until fully incorporated.

6 Slice the remaining pear and
arrange in a fan pattern on the base
of the tin.

7 Spoon the cake mixture into the tin
and cook in a preheated oven.
150˚C/300˚F/Gas Mark 2, for 1¹⁄₄ –
1¹⁄₂ hours or until cooked through.

8 Remove the cake from the oven
and leave to cool in the tin for
10 minutes.

9 Turn the cake out on to a wire
cooling rack and drizzle with honey.
Leave to cool completely, then cut into
slices to serve.

COOK'S TIP

To test if the cake is cooked through,
insert a skewer into the centre – if it
comes out clean the cake is cooked. If
not, return the cake to the oven and
test at frequent intervals.

Chocolate Fudge Pudding

This pudding has a hidden surprise when cooked as it separates
to give a rich chocolate sauce at the bottom of the dish.

Serves 4

50 g/1¾ oz vegetarian margarine, plus
extra for greasing

75 g/2¾ oz soft light brown sugar

2 eggs, beaten

350 ml/12 fl oz milk

50 g/1¾ oz chopped walnuts

40 g/1½ oz plain flour

2 tbsp cocoa powder

icing sugar and cocoa,
to dust

1 Lightly grease a 1 litre/1¾ pint
ovenproof dish.

2 Cream the margarine and sugar
until fluffy and beat in the eggs.

3 Gradually stir in the milk and add
the walnuts.

4 Sieve the flour and cocoa powder
into the mixture and fold in gently
until well mixed.

5 Spoon the mixture into the dish
and cook in a preheated oven at
180°C/350°F/Gas Mark 4 for 35–40
minutes or until the sponge is cooked.
Dust with icing sugar and cocoa
powder and serve.

COOK'S VARIATION

Add 1–2 tbsp brandy or rum to the
mixture for a slightly alcoholic pudding,
or 1–2 tbsp orange juice for a child-
friendly version.

Passion Cake

Decorating this moist, rich carrot cake with sugared flowers lifts
it into the celebration class. It is a perfect choice for Easter.

Serves 8-10

150 ml/¼ pint corn oil

175 g/6 oz golden caster sugar

4 tbsp natural yogurt

3 eggs, plus 1 extra yolk

1 tsp vanilla flavouring

125 g/4½ oz walnut pieces, chopped

175 g/6 oz carrots, grated

1 banana, mashed

175 g/6 oz plain
flour

90 g/3 oz fine oatmeal

1 tsp bicarbonate of soda

1 tsp baking powder

1 tsp ground cinnamon

½ tsp salt

FROSTING

150 g/5½ oz low-fat
soft cheese

4 tbsp natural yogurt

90 g/3 oz icing sugar

1 tsp grated lemon rind

2 tsp lemon juice

DECORATION

primroses and violets

1 egg white, lightly beaten

40 g/1½ oz caster sugar

1 Grease and line a 23 cm/9 inch
round cake tin. Beat the oil, sugar,
yogurt, eggs, egg yolk and vanilla. Beat
in the walnuts, carrot and banana. Sift
the remaining ingredients and beat
into the mixture.

2 Pour the mixture into the tin and
level the surface. Bake in a preheated
oven, 180°C/350°F/Gas Mark 4, for 1½

hours or until firm. Insert a skewer
into the centre: it should come out
clean. Cool in the tin for 15 minutes,
then transfer to a wire rack.

3 To make the frosting, beat together
the cheese and yogurt. Sift in the icing
sugar and stir in the lemon rind and
juice. Spread over the top and sides of

the cake. To prepare the decoration,
dip the flowers quickly in the beaten
egg white, then sprinkle with caster
sugar to cover. Place well apart on
baking parchment. Leave in a warm,
dry place for several hours until they
are dry and crisp. Arrange the flowers
on top of the cake.

Index